WITH MY HEAD IN THE CLOUDS
AND
STARS IN MY EYES

STORIES ABOUT IRAN AND ELSEWHERE

JOOBIN BEKHRAD

About the Author

Joobin Bekhrad is the author of numerous books of prose and poetry (*Coming Down Again*; *Lovers of Light*; *Elsewhere*; and *The Quatrains of Omar Khayyam*). His writings have also appeared in publications such as *The New York Times*, *The Washington Post*, *The Economist*, *Forbes*, *The Financial Times*, *The Guardian*, and the *Columbia Journal* (whose Online Guest Editor he served as in 2016), as well as on the BBC's website and in various art-related books.

In 2015, Joobin was granted an International Award for Art Criticism (IAAC) by London's Royal College of Art. His work has also been recognised by individuals like acclaimed historian Tom Holland and Simon Napier-Bell, as well as publications including *Monocle*.

Acknowledgments

Aside from the luminaries who inspired many of the stories in this collection, I would like to offer – in alphabetical order – my sincere thanks to a number of exceptional individuals: Sultan Sooud Al Qassemi, for his hospitality in Dubai and Toronto; Arash Ashkar, for the beautiful artwork that graces this book's cover; Sassan and Maria Behnam Bakhtiar for a lovely time (and some wonderful wine) in Saint-Jean- Cap-Ferrat; Giovanna Calvenzi, for her input in *Iran, 1970* (and Riccarda Mandrini, for putting us in touch); Dr Manoutchehr Eskandari-Qajar, for his constant support and encouragement; Hushidar Mortezaie, for his touching introduction; Henry Kim, for introducing me to the late, great Abbas Kiarostami; Mona Paad, for her kindness during my visit to Parviz Tanavoli's Tehran studio; and Behzad Sadeghi, for sharing *Persian Heart, Northern Soul* with the brilliant Kourosh Yaghmaei.

I must also thank my father, Shahdad Bekhrad, for ingraining in me the amazing stories of his childhood and introducing to me my uncle Mehrdad, whom I never got the chance to know, as well as Sadra Tehranchian, my maternal grandfather, for his colourful recollections of his father, Sheykh Kazem Tehranchian.

Contents

Introduction
Hushidar Mortezaie

Joobin Bekhrad once called me 'an ambassador of all things Iranian'. He must have been describing himself. He is a kindred spirit, as he shares with me an undying love for Iran and has devoted himself to sharing with the world the beauty and splendour of a culture rooted in good thoughts, good words, and good deeds. This sublime collection of stories and essays, in which Bekhrad spins his golden prose again, is only one of many examples of his passion and dedication.

In his travels as a stateless nomad meandering the globe, Bekhrad searches for – and discovers – a path leading him back to the beginning, to the 'Gate of All Nations', to the navel of the world: Iran. In doing so, he pens ideas and memories, recalling the minutiae of the moments he has lived and imagined. The welcoming fragrance of a hyacinth's blossoming, psychedelic paisley tapestries infused with frankincense smoke, the essence of the late Persian demigod Farrokh Bulsara, and the caustic smog that has long choked Tehran all rise forth from his pages. Bekhrad knots words to create an ornate tableau of life, much like a rug weaver's hands tying together the twisting threads of a Persian carpet. Personal stories that read like fragments of an autobiography are interwoven with tales of iconic Iranian luminaries and intellectuals alongside scholarly essays about the many treasures of our beloved Iran. The result is a mixture of seventies glamour, laments for child martyrs and fallen icons, and the bacchanalia of drunken orgies soaked in intoxicating verse.

Poetry is the blood that runs from Bekhrad's veins onto paper and that tells a history of lives and experiences. His stories, which read more like graceful *ghazals*, seem to have been set to a Stones record. One can almost imagine a groupie, resplendent with a glittering headpiece and kohl-rimmed eyes, reclining in a haze of cigarette smoke on the back of a tour bus en route to the Shiraz-Persepolis Festival of Arts. The pieces in his book create images like dreams, which come together to form an epic postmodern tale about a homeland people like him and me shall return to – if only in the most golden and poignant of visions.

While the pieces in this collection vary in their settings, from 'Tehranto' and Tehran to the streets of Paris and Prague, they unite an entire population of scattered Iranian émigrés. With the unfolding of every chapter, Bekhrad lyrically tells his own story, as well as those of pioneers and icons in the sphere of contemporary Iranian arts and culture. A filmmaker, a philosopher, a poet, a sculptor, a rock and roller, a queen: the heroes Bekhrad writes about give Iranians like me a key to their misplaced souls. These luminaries represent much more than fame and celebrity; their lives, dotted with greatness and failure, and told through Bekhrad's unique voice, allow people like me to travel back to periods in Iranian history they never experienced, and that have something to say about the present. The works of tragic heroes like Sadegh Hedayat are eternal, and abound with sparks of hope for new audiences decades later.

* * *

In *I Want to Cry Like Soraya*, we read about gifts of art and beauty from Iran and the crushing fates of those who bore them. Soraya Esfandiary Bakhtiari was unmatched in her beauty, so haunting and exquisite. Comparisons to Western icons like Ingrid Bergman and Ava Gardner kept popping up, but Soraya was Soraya, and her gaze seared through the headlines and into the heart of the Shah. On her wedding day, she appeared in a Christian Dior gown designed when Dior was 'Dior' – and that is exactly how I imagine a queen to be. Although the Shah offered to keep her as a wife after it was clear that the two wouldn't be able to have children, Soraya didn't stand for the injustice. 'She wouldn't play second fiddle to anyone, neither in this life or the next', writes Bekhrad in his piece. I was, and always will be a part of 'team Soraya'.

The most heartbreaking loss to Iranian culture for me, however, was the suicide of the greatest writer and intellectual we've ever had: Sadegh Hedayat. Hedayat's works, both surrealist and realist, are modern masterpieces of Persian literature. They challenged censors at every step, doing away with the past and introducing new ideas that will forever remain timeless. Hedayat was a true revolutionary and romantic (and dandy), who never pandered to anyone and spoke his truths. Alas, his struggles with anti-intellectuals and those ignorant of Iran's greatness proved too much for Hedayat to deal with, and, in the end, he finally freed himself of 'knowing too much' by gassing himself to death in his Paris apartment. Decades later, other Iranian visionaries like Abbas Kiarostami would also master the art of eluding censors as Hedayat did, by speaking in metaphor and saying so much with so little.

Elsewhere, in *Persian Heart, Northern Soul*, Bekhrad eloquently captures the spirit of his university days in London, while also adding another dimension to the aura surrounding Kourosh Yaghmaei's beloved *Gol-e Yakh* (*Ice Flower*). In *Poet of Persia*, Bekhrad recounts not a memory, but a meeting in the flesh with an Iranian icon, this time Parviz Tanavoli, the 'father of modern Iranian sculpture'. I'll never forget the time I visited the Tehran Museum of Contemporary Art in 2003, a few weeks after *Norooz*, the Iranian New Year. I had no idea Tanavoli was having an exhibition there, and walked towards a towering, glistening *Heech* (*Nothingness*) sculpture of his. I was mesmerised and elated, yet silent, as I felt 'everything and nothing', as Bekhrad writes. Tanavoli reminds me of those

Iranians who make up the salt of the earth, as well as my father, whose idea of *mardanegi* (which roughly translates to 'manliness') was likewise characterised by decency, ethics, and generosity. Men like Tanavoli and my father fought against injustice and did their part in forging futures; and in this sense, Tanavoli is a true Farhad, sculpting his ideas with conviction, craft, and authenticity.

* * *

Sometimes artists cross beyond the threshold separating mortals from deities, and come to stand for so much more than mere individuals. Few in Iranian culture have enjoyed the statuses of those like Cyrus the Great, King of Kings; but, as Bekhrad mentions in *The First Time Ever I Saw Your Face*, 'Cyrus is the Father, and Googoosh the Daughter, if there's ever been one'. I so believe that. In the story, Bekhrad writes about his first encounter with the diva in a way that makes me feel as if we were twin brothers born in different parts of the world. I had an almost identical 'love at first sight' experience. Both Bekhrad and I discovered her at a very young age through VHS tapes and cassettes either brought over from Iran, or purchased from Iranian supermarkets abroad. When Bekhrad first saw Googoosh in an explosion of colour and kitsch on the television, something came alive. 'Memories of a previous life were awakened; I'd been there all along, and through

Googoosh, the past came rushing forth in vivid colour', he recalls.

My first discovery of Googoosh – also on a television screen – laid part of the groundwork for my life and career. Her look constantly morphed in a chameleon-like manner, and with each style more glamorous than the last, she put the likes of Loulou de la Falaise to shame. I have always been enamoured of self-expression through style and art. Many of my childhood daydreams were the result of the fairy-tale high of afternoons during which I watched episodes of the pre-Revolution *Rangarang* (*Colourful*) show that had found their way to the US. I was hypnotised by starlets in the most dazzling disco couture on stages that looked more like sequinned mosques with their sparkling patterns, a sort of camp counterpart to the mirror-work of Monir Farmanfarmaian. On the centre of those stages, ruling supreme, was a glittering beam of light that danced and sang, making the hairs of my chubby-cheeked nine-year-old self stand on end. Electrified, my already large eyes dilated to the sight of this being dripping in silver bugle beads, refracting light, and stopping time. She moved and shimmied as she sang songs like *Khalvat* (*Emptiness*), her voice so melancholic and soothing, yet so strong, reaching out into the stars and back. The light was familiar; I had known it from before. It was the light of Mithras, of the heroes of Pasargad and ancient Iran, shining in my soul.

My father was watching, sweetly snapping his fingers behind me on our plaid wool couch. 'Azar,' he said, 'look at your son! He hasn't moved since Googoosh started singing.' I wasn't paying attention to my parents (or anything else), until I heard the click-clack of my mom's burgundy boots I had secretly borrowed to complete my Wonder Woman outfit. 'No one even compared to her', Maman said. I've heard those words from her mouth over and over again since then; even today, we bond over her videos on Persian satellite television, the only difference being that Maman's voice is a little frailer, a little softer. Exhausted from having worked so hard to raise a family, chasing the American dream, and losing her sweetheart of fifty years – my Baba – her pride and fire still blaze with grace.

As Maman sat down next to Baba behind me, the close-ups showed Googoosh's face framed by a glitzy sequin knit with beads and tassels that swayed as she danced. Her large drunken eyes, their lids painted in her signature metallic green, provided a window to the essence of her being. As the next video played, I still sat transfixed. The song Googoosh was singing to this time was *Talagh* (*Divorce*). I had no idea that what she was wearing – a light pink chiffon dress with cut sleeves draping across her body – would become the inspiration for an outfit I would design for a runway show twenty-one years later, called 'Biba Googoosh'. Googoosh was more 'Biba' than Barbara Hulanicki's Biba ever was, with all its opium disco lights and deco pop. I never realised as I was working that I was taking all my inspirations and fantasies to create my own look based on the figure of that strong Iranian woman. Not only was it her style that influenced me, but her life story, too. Googoosh had experienced, amidst the glory and glamour, so much tragedy and sadness, including being banned from singing in Iran; but she nonetheless survived and stayed around to sing and create, embodying the quintessential Iranian spirit of undying strength and resilience also championed by Maman. I was so entranced by Googoosh that, in the late nineties and early 2000s, many referred to me as a small, thirty-something, male Googoosh. They didn't understand what she meant to me, and how important a symbol she was to many like me in the Iranian diaspora. Now, the same people are trying to imitate Googoosh.

* * *

The majority of the individuals Bekhrad has written about are Iranian, but there are some exceptions to the rule. Bekhrad has included a tribute to Turkey's Yashar Kemal on account of his Kurdish/Iranic roots. There are also stories about David Bowie, the Moroccan singer Hindi Zahra, and an exhibition of contemporary Arab art, which he has included as he delves deep into his Iranian identity in them. Reading the stories, it was impossible not to find a part of my own Iranian

DNA within each paragraph. The passages about Bekhrad's teenage years in Toronto, in which he started becoming more aware of his Iranian heritage, and Sassan Behnam Bakhtiar's upbringing in Paris and Tehran after the devastation of the Iran-Iraq War mirrored my own experiences as a proud little boy in California romanticising a faraway place. The Iran of my dreams was the place where Zoroastrianism preached love and righteousness, and from where the Safavids gave the world high heels.

In writing about Iranian culture, Bekhrad often looks to its influence on the world stage and its contributions to civilisation. *Of Bandits and Popinjays,* his essay about Persian episodes in twentieth-century Western rock and roll history, is of particular importance to me as he writes with affection in it about an icon we have both long admired: Farrokh Bulsara, a.k.a. 'Freddie Mercury'. Farrokh's brazen sexuality was a 'fuck you' to the establishment, and his legacy will always remain in the heart of this shy little Iranian boy who was bullied for not being masculine enough and looking different. I'll never forget those days in school, learning about people like Farrokh. 'I'll always walk around like a Persian popinjay,' he once said, 'and no one's gonna stop me, honey!' In the same spirit, when it came to speaking about Iran, you couldn't shut me up. I was rather quiet, but would go around telling my classmates that Iran's Qajars had popularised unibrows long before Frida Kahlo. This game of 'we did it first' may seem trivial, but when the media consistently portrays your homeland as savage and backwards, you feel a desire to challenge that narrative.

As a child, primetime television inundated me with headlines about the Hostage Crisis and images of denim jackets with pins of Mickey Mouse giving Iran the finger. Similar ephemera even found their ways into schoolyards where Iranian-American children played and were tormented for being 'the enemy', myself included. The pressure to assimilate had destructive effects on my self-esteem as a child, as well as on my livelihood as a designer later on. Middle Eastern culture, particularly that of Iran, was considered 'un-American' as a result of events like the Hostage Crisis and – strangely – 9/11.

The only way I knew how to battle the racism and hatred I encountered was through art and a love for Iran. Art gave me the power to hold my head up high with dignity to show that us Iranians would resist – and thrive. I manifested my reactions in fashion design and visual art, unveiling a new Iranian look in the nineties and 2000s, designing ostentatiously Iranian outfits for the likes of Brad Pitt, Madonna, Sarah Jessica Parker, and Beyoncé. My collections included postmodern Iranian princesses storming runways in militant gowns upon which I scribbled revolutionary slogans in Persian calligraphy. Those 'Googooshettes' stood tall in their *hejabs* with their arched unibrows, dazzling in ornate headpieces, silk chiffon, leather biker jackets adorned with Hafez-inspired Persian miniatures, and high-heeled, curly-toed cowboy boots that I used to explore the cowboys and Indians game of 'otherness' in art. I used my conceptual pop background, informed by the life I'd left behind and the longing I had to create images that blurred distinctions between high and low, haute and camp, East and West. It was about unity and rejecting exclusivity and segregation, which had been at the heart of all the pain I'd dealt with growing up. I had to create a new home to heal what was missing, a hybrid of both cultures, like myself. I created a new conceptual language of pop for a new generation to relate to and through which they could celebrate their Iranian heritage. Terms like 'weapons of mass destruction' and 'Axis of Evil' were turned upside down and used as armour to reject stereotypes using their very sources.

* * *

Within this beautifully written collection of stories and essays are deeply touching episodes that have the ability to unite the nomadic souls of Iranians the world over. I was moved – and brought to tears – reading what appeared at many times to be a reflection of my entire life, in which I've wandered about starry-eyed and confused about where I belong. There are also the tragedies my family and people have faced, and still face. In *Children of the Revolution*, Bekhrad's gift of inspiring is evident through the pure emotion he channels and the grace of his voice. His endearing and touching stories about his paternal grandparents, Maman Aziz and Baba Nosrat, tenderly reveal a very personal and private side, and remind me of my own incredible love for my late father, Vali Khan, who lived through the Revolution and under various regimes until finally being uprooted from his beloved Iran. His life was about humanity, service, and a pure love for Iran. He was proud of being Iranian no matter what anyone said or did. His love defied the Revolution, the Peacock Throne, the martyrs, the question of the *hejab*, the despair of the 'burnt generation' (my generation), and the great pains and losses of the Iranian people, past and present. It was, as Bekhrad writes in the story, '... draped in red, white, and green, shining as brightly as the sun'. It was not only about love and pride with Baba, but also being able to move forward while still looking back. We Iranians must, he believed, return to our roots and speak with pride about our heritage, and keep alive the magic of our myths and legends. We must know who we are; we must know our brilliant history and infuse it with the hope of what the future can, through our love for Iran, be.

For my Baba, Valiollah Mortezaie (1930 – 2014), who taught me to hold my head up high and be proud of who I was.

Persian Heart, Northern Soul

I stepped out of the piss-stained elevator, my hands burning in the pockets of my blue jeans. Beneath my beery breath, I was whistling a piano melody that had been swirling and sparkling about in my mind for days. I looked over my shoulder to make sure no one was around; all I could see from behind the blurred window of the apartment door was a ragtag band of children kicking around a ball in the side-street outside. I tried to remember the words to a bit of the song that Kaveh had been singing minutes earlier to the sound of cracking pistachio shells, but couldn't. He knew all the words to those Persian love songs, that Kaveh. Far away from home, on the sticky streets of the city, he'd often put his arm around my neck and sing some ditty or other, while I'd try to stifle a massive grin. Ah, autumn! We wondered then about the mess we'd gotten ourselves into, but knew, somehow, that everything would be alright; for there was always the local boozer to slip into, spill the beans, and pour our hearts out, and always the voice of Kourosh.

Walking about on the sooty pavement outside, I realised my shoes didn't fit. It looked like it was about to rain, but something kept dragging me onwards. I ditched the goddamned bus, full of glassy-eyed hoodlums chewing away on fried ordure, and walked on, my feet shifting about in my kicks. Passing by a Turkish greengrocer's plastered with advertisements for calling cards, my stomach sank; I felt an inexplicable anxiety, a dull weight, press down upon me like the 'empty mass' Kourosh had sung about. I didn't know why; the worst was behind me. My heart wasn't in anyone's hands, and I could once again confide in the sun. It was a new semester and a new year, but it was also April. There was still time left; anything could have happened. It was also a Sunday. What would tomorrow bring? Where would I be? I didn't know, just as I didn't know what I was doing then, or where I was going. Making up other words in lieu for the original lyrics, all I could do was sing along to that haunting melody when nobody was looking.

* * *

I was sitting atop my windowsill one evening, all dressed up (in a weathered T-shirt) and ready to go out for dinner with my grandparents. I could hear Grandma in the other room squabbling with Grandpa over his choice of clothing. 'Leave me alone! I want to go back to Tehran!' I could hear him moan against the creak of a closet door. I turned up the volume of my record player and looked outside at the lone tree standing on the other side of the street, and the lamp that always glowed an incandescent pink, but for a few seconds, before turning yellow; I wouldn't have missed those moments for the world that evening. In the neighbouring apartment building, people were cooking dinner and watching football, and outside, the man with the poorboy cap was having his usual eight o'clock smoke. I fixed my gaze on the glowing embers of his cigarette, and, just as Kourosh uttered the first verses of *Ice Flower*, our eyes met for a second. *Sorrow has made a nest between your beautiful eyes.* 'Joobin! Have you gotten dressed yet?' '*Baleh, baleh …*'

At the dinner table, somewhere in the West End, those piercing, echoing licks buzzed about in my ears, and I couldn't stop thinking about that white guitar. It occurred to me then that the first guitar I'd ever seen was white, too. I don't remember much of my cousin's wedding in London as an eleven-year-old, except for the band that kept to itself in the background, performing a set of inoffensive numbers to an oblivious crowd. Despite the all-round banality of the whole affair, and, thinking the guitarist the very antithesis of rock and roll, I still couldn't take my eyes off of his Telecaster. *Norooz* had already passed, and my birthday was months away, so I knew it would be a while before I'd be able to get my little hands on such a thing, which I wanted more than anything else in the world. *If only they'd get me a white electric guitar,* I thought, *I'd get Mum and Dad as many A-pluses as they could possibly wish for.* Shortly afterwards, I resolved to do away with the piano (just as I'd dropped out of Persian classes) and sling a six-string – and I knew exactly which guitar I'd convince my parents to buy me: Brian Jones' white

15

Vox teardrop. But that April afternoon, it was Kourosh's white Stratocaster I was daydreaming about; I didn't want to be a Rolling Stone. I wanted to be a Persian rock and roll star.

* * *

Passing by Super Persia near Archway Station, I missed Grandma more than ever. I thought about popping in to pick up some *sangak* bread and tea, but didn't have the patience to chitchat with Jamshid, the smooth-talking owner who always managed to sell us things we didn't need. I thought about what Grandma might have been doing then. She was probably watching BBC Persian whilst engrossed in a telephone marathon with her cousin Mehran. I knew that, in an hour or so, Grandpa would bring out his chequered backgammon board, and he and Grandma would go at it for hours. *Three and four. Two and two. Koor koor. Look at this luck!* Cyrus, Cyrus. My clothes were sopping wet, but I didn't care; your song was on the tip of my tongue, your guitar ringing in my being. I had left behind sordid Holloway Road, and had stopped thinking about my shoes. Even the sky looked different that day. From behind the slab of grey, engulfing all, shone forth a sheet of light while the rain poured down. High on a hill, I looked in vain for the little fox that usually skulked about in the dead of night, and stopped to regard the glistening creepers on a fence and a swollen branch swaying in the thick, heavy air. Grandpa used to say that his teachers would make sure the cherry branches they'd batter their tiny feet with as schoolchildren were wet, for added effect. In the back of my mind, I heard the rattle and twang of an old *dotar*, and wished it was *Norooz* again.

It was then that I realised I was a northern soul, and would always be one. I recalled the first time I saw the Caspian Sea. Having passed through the winding mountains, I awoke in the backseat of an old *Paykan* taxicab, my head comfortably nestled in my friend's lap. My back was moist with perspiration, and the air felt strange. I looked at it with incredulity, thinking a thousand thoughts. *The Caspian Sea. Hyrcania. The land of my forefathers.* Yes, those coruscating shades of grey, that deep green, that blushing pink – I knew them all too well. I saw what Kourosh had seen in the rains he so often sang about, in the bittersweet spring. All of my melancholy and misgivings became tinged with a sort of ashen bliss as I stood there in Whitehall Park, wishing that April would never end, and Monday would never come.

Spotting the honeyed glow of my bedroom lamp in the distance, I smiled at the thought of playing truant the next day and running down to Denmark Street to catch a glimpse of Kourosh's magical white guitar – after, of course, snagging some sneakers that fit.

7/19/2016

Joobin Bekhrad

Where the Boys Go

I was only too happy to be leaving Prague; it's not exactly my kind of place. At the same time, I wasn't particularly looking forward to the nosebleed flight to the other end of the world awaiting me. What on earth was I doing there, anyway? Even I didn't know. The damned pink walls of my hotel room were beginning to curse me, and the AC had long before done a number on me.

I awoke with a burning throat at around a quarter to three in the morning, not hearing a sound on the cobblestone streets below, draped in deepest black. Not even a hot shower could bring me to my senses, and, after awkwardly slipping on my black jeans (why do I always bring so many pairs when I only ever wear one?), I flicked on the television out of utter boredom. I was expecting the usual: Brexit, Baghdad, Dhaka, Medina, ISIS here, ISIS there. *What a week*, I thought to myself, as I coolly flipped through the channels before my thumb stopped clicking.

There was no mistaking those shades, that equanimity. No news is good news, and all news is bad news. *Kiarostami has gone, too.* I was thinking in Persian, on the verge of waxing sentimental; yet, I felt numb, just as I did when I'd heard about the attacks of the past week. I wanted to feel an outpouring of emotion, a pang, a shiver – *something*. No matter how hard I tried, I couldn't find anything within, save a gaping hollow. Was it because I'd grown indifferent to death, or simply because I was no longer the child who'd once thought his heroes immortal? Death for me used to be an event, a spectacle; I'd be stunned for days, trying to make sense of everything. My world was quieter as a boy, and such untimely demises left a mark of some kind, no matter how small. Now, it seems as if they're just headlines, other pieces of news for journalists to scramble over like a pack of rabid dogs. For whatever reason, I remembered another one of my heroes, the Persian mystic Attar of Neyshapur, and his sheer indifference at his death at the hands of the Mongols. A disdain for the faithless wheel of heaven aside, I wondered then whether it was the twenty-first century or the thirteenth. The hordes of Hulagu could have been sweeping through Bohemia at that very moment, and I wouldn't have so much as batted an eyelash.

All I knew then was that a part of Iran had died, and in turn, a part of me. *What a week,* I kept saying to myself, over and over again, trying to ignore the Czech pop songs buzzing on the taxi radio on the way to the airport.

* * *

I didn't grow up with Kiarostami's films. I discovered Abbas Kiarostami long after he'd become *Kiarostami*, during the same time that I began devouring everything having to do with Iranian culture. I vaguely remember visiting the Film Museum off of Vali-ye Asr Avenue in Tehran with my friend one hot summer's day, when I was around sixteen years old. I had no idea who the man in the sunglasses was, only that he was of significance where Iranian cinema was concerned. To people like my friend (a film buff now working in the industry in Iran), directors like Kiarostami, Mohsen Makhmalbaf, and Dariush Mehrjui were demigods, not mere mortals; they had set the gold standard for Iranian arthouse cinema, and all and sundry took their cues from them. I remember hearing Kiarostami's name more than anyone else's though; it was he, apparently, who headed the pantheon of Iran's great post-Revolution directors. It therefore only seemed natural that, when beginning my foray into the seemingly endless ocean of Iranian cinema, I'd begin with his films. I hadn't a clue what I was doing, but as long as Kiarostami's name was on the tin, I knew I was in good company.

* * *

Some years later, as a second-year university student in Toronto, I would stock up on all kinds of Iranian films – black-and-white classics, *Film-Farsi*, masterpieces, and outright trash. It didn't matter what the subject was; as long as the film had to do with Iran, I was interested. I can't remember most of what I watched; as I'm writing now, images are passing by my eyes in a blur. *Gheysar* was, and always will be my all-time favourite film, but I also vividly recall the works of Kiarostami. I began with the titles with which he rose to international fame, and worked my way backwards. The classic *Khaneh-ye Doost Kojast?* (*Where is the Friend's Home?*) and *Ta'm-e Gilas* (*Taste of Cherry*) were my first introductions to his art and philosophy. Admittedly, his signature extended shots of figures slowly receding into the distance tried my patience as a teenager, but for some reason, I nonetheless felt myself continuously drawn to the pictures he would paint. I wasn't watching arthouse cinema for the sake of it, or to have something clever to say at a cocktail party, but rather to learn more about my country, my language, and my people. Watching Kiarostami's films, I felt as if I actually were in northern Iran, walking alongside his innocent children, or in the backseat of a *Paykan* on the squalid streets of Tehran. As with the earlier films of Jafar Panahi, what at first struck me the most was Kiarostami's brazen honesty: he wasn't sensationalising or criticising (openly, at least) anything – he was telling it like it was. I saw his films not as spectacles, but – recalling the earliest definition of films – moving pictures that afforded me, one who had always looked at his motherland from afar, a glimpse of what it meant to be Iranian. If Ferdowsi had nailed it with the *Shahnameh* (*Book of Kings*), his thirty-year-long labour of love and paean to Iran,

Joobin Bekhrad

Kiarostami, perhaps, achieved the same behind his camera, centuries later.

As a student, I used to watch Kiarostami's films on and off. I admired them, but never considered myself an ardent follower, unlike a Korean professor of mine. Things took a turn, however, when I somehow discovered his early pre-Revolution films, which he had made for the Centre for the Intellectual Development of Children and Young Adults. Watching *Mosafer* (*The Traveller*), *Lebas-i Barayeh Aroosi* (*A Wedding Suit*), *Zang-e Tafrih* (*Breaktime*), and *Nan va Kucheh* (*Bread and Alley*) was love at first sight. The cinematography wasn't as refined, and they didn't carry messages as weighty as those in the Palme d'Or-winning *Taste of Cherry*, but they spoke to me more than any of his other films, no matter how many awards they'd won. For the first time, I felt myself caring for the characters in a film; I could empathise with them. I inherited their joys, fears, and sorrows, and all the excitement of a naughty boy looking for a bit of fun in the big city. My heart sank during the final scene of *The Traveller*, in which Kiarostami's boy hero (who else?) saw all his dreams and schemes to attend a football match in Tehran amount to naught, as all those little stubs fluttered about in the wind; and, watching *A Wedding Suit*, I couldn't help but remember all the times I'd looked at my father's closet in awe, trying on his clothes and never minding that his blazers were three sizes too big for me. I loved those little boys, for whom I'd cheer behind my television screen. I wanted to tell them to ditch their thoughts of homework and grown-ups, and to stay forever young – exactly like the director himself.

* * *

I've never cared much for eulogies; I fail to take them seriously or assign a modicum of honesty to their authors. Call me a pessimist, a sceptic, whatever. I haven't read any of the tributes to Kiarostami yet, but I have glossed over some of the titles being attributed to him: 'Father of Iranian Cinema', 'genius', 'one of the world's greatest directors'. I'll leave such things to the critics. I always regarded Kiarostami as someone to look up to not because he was a great director (as I said, I never watched his films for the sake of great cinema), but – more than anything else – because he saw the world through the eyes of a child. If his films became somewhat more 'weighty' with time, it was only because Kiarostami had grown wiser with age – not older. While he was known for his use of non-professional child actors who barely knew him, the subject of children extended far beyond the surface of his craft. I wasn't only witnessing children running about, trying to give back their friends' notebooks before the next school day or playing hooky; I was thinking like a child, wandering like a child, relishing the simplest pleasures of life with unparalleled pleasure like a child, and shivering in my little trousers like one.

That the child in Kiarostami continued to live on and dream, rather than be quelled by the passing of time and the death of innocence is, to me, his greatest feat bar none. Just as I love my rock and roll stars because they never grew up, so too do I love artists like Kiarostami. Marc Bolan, Antoine Saint-Exupéry, Abbas Kiarostami – they are all but variations on a theme, the starry-eyed brethren of the Lost Boys.

* * *

When I was told Kiarostami was in town last November, I didn't know what to think. I've always been wary of meeting those whom I admire, as I never know whether or not they'll live up to the images I've conjured in my head. My first thought is usually that they'll turn out to be assholes. As well, I don't ever have anything to say to such people, either. *I mean, what would I say to him?* I thought at the time. *Love your films, mister?* Or, like someone I once knew had said to Rod Stewart upon bumping into him in a hotel elevator, 'You're doing a good job'? What does one say in such situations? I certainly didn't want to spew out proverbial Persian sweet-nothings or try to affect the airs of a savant. I even thought for a moment that it would be better if I skipped the event altogether. I'm glad, for once, I didn't.

I was due to meet a friend at a talk by Kiarostami at the headquarters of the Toronto International

Film Festival downtown, and he'd requested I bring him some copies of my magazine. Afterwards, I handed my friend the magazines I'd brought along and said I'd be heading home. He wanted me to meet Kiarostami, but, perhaps after being hounded by fans inside the theatre who kept asking him if he could remember them, the man in black had slipped away out the back door of the building. Upon realising this, my friend told me there was a dinner being held in his honour just a block away that he was hosting, and suggested I join them. 'OK', I said, noticing it had begun snowing, and wondering why on earth I'd decided, out of all nights, to wear my new suede shoes.

There he was, standing right in front of me, sans hangers-on and acolytes. I thought it would be strange if I didn't say anything to him, yet, at the same time, found myself at a loss for words. If my friend hadn't introduced me to him, I probably would have remained silent all night. I can't recall exactly what he said, but my companion mentioned my magazine and the sorts of things I was involved with. I anticipated that my encounter would end that very moment; to my surprise, however, Kiarostami struck up a conversation and flashed his pearly whites. I handed him a copy of the magazine in one of *REORIENT* 's 'Sex, Drugs, and *Gol-o-Bolbol*' tote bags, and before we headed to the table, simply told him that I had long loved his films and was very happy to meet him. *Yeah, he's alright,* I thought, walking upstairs, feeling fuzzy in the afterglow.

At one end of the table, I espied Atom Egoyan. Sitting directly across from me was Kiarostami, with whom I merely exchanged glances and smiled every now and then. Myriad conversations were happening, and, for whatever reason, I and the people around me began talking about Freddie Mercury. The bizarreness of it all soon began to sink in, and, at one point, I turned to another friend beside me and asked, 'Is this for real?' It has been said that in Kiarostami's films, the ordinary and mundane become *extra*ordinary. That evening, it was exactly the opposite; there I was, sitting across from a man deemed one of the greatest-ever directors in the history of cinema, talking about rock and roll as if he weren't even there: the extraordinary had become unsettlingly ordinary. Perhaps it was because of the way the man carried himself; he largely kept to himself, and, though the sole reason of the gathering, wasn't asking for any attention whatsoever. With such an oeuvre as his, anyone else would have been content with simply enjoying their spiced chicken, too.

Minutes turned into hours. I hadn't yet met Atom Egoyan, but, being incredibly gracious, he came around to say goodbye as I was busy downing a mouthful of saffron-scented rice. I also said farewell to the person who had earlier on interviewed Kiarostami in the theatre, and who was noticeably peeved by the fact that I didn't know he was the Director of the Film Festival. Oh well. Outside, I shook hands again with the man behind the shades beneath falling snowflakes, hoping I'd see him again. The restaurant had closed for the evening, and a taxi was waiting to take El Padre back to his hotel. Just as I was about to leave, he began feeling around in his pockets with a look of agitation. 'My magazine! I forgot my magazine …' Thankfully it was still where he had left it in the restaurant, which opened its doors again for us. 'Uh, *befarmaid*', I said, blushing as I handed him the tote with the magazine in it. '*Khoda negahdar*' were the last words I said to him before he hopped into the orange cab and I began brushing away the little white crystals that had settled in the thicket atop my head.

* * *

'Once you're dead, you're made for life', Hendrix once said. If there's anything that brings consolation to me now, it's that Kiarostami was one of those rare artists who were celebrated as luminaries for a great deal of their own lifetimes. 'Ah, Iran! You guys make great movies', my friends would often say to me. They most probably hadn't heard of *Gheysar*, and certainly not any of my beloved Nasser Malek-Motiee flicks. Hell, they probably didn't even know where Iran was on a map; but a mere mention of *Where is the Friend's Home?* would usually get a few nods, at the very least. Being heaped with praise by industry giants, film festivals, and connoisseurs is one thing, but being a household name in the unlikeliest of places is another. Iranian cinema flourished outside the career of Kiarostami, at home and abroad, as it will continue to; but to merely say that Kiarostami helped make Iranian cinema the darling it is today is a wild understatement.

On the way back home, high up in the skies, I thought about how I would remember Kiarostami as I battled a fever. None of the many titles or laurels he garnered will come to mind, nor will any of the accolades given him by his contemporaries. The name 'Abbas Kiarostami' won't get me thinking about the greatest this or that, or the pioneer of such-and-such. Rather, I will recall the simple and kind man who opened windows into my country and culture in ways no one else could. A man who deepened my love for my people, and gave me a new understanding of what it meant to be Iranian. A man who, with his childlike heart and soul, reminded me of the overwhelming beauty of life, which can always be ours and is always waiting to be beheld by our eyes – if only we open them.

7/11/2016

In memory of Abbas Kiarostami (1940 – 2016).

Poet of Persia

After taking a final swig of *doogh*, haphazardly gathering my sundry belongings into my weathered canvas satchel, and kissing my friend three times on the cheeks, I rush down a rickety flight of stairs to a picturesque summer scene in Deh-e Vanak, a sleepy hamlet but a short drive from the mania of Tehran's Vanak Square. Brushing shoulders with a covey of weary-eyed mechanics, their gasoline-smeared faces wizened by the beating sun and heartache in equal amounts, and traversing the pothole-ridden thoroughfare with a characteristically Western trepidation, I struggle to find my taxi driver amongst the scores of moribund *Paykans* and sooty Peugeot 206s. By a stroke of ill luck, the traffic is unusually awful, and I'm already half-an-hour late for another get-together with an artist. This artist, however, is somewhat different from the others I know, whom I usually meet in the tawny-hued lobby of the Hotel Homa – the 'Old Sheraton', as those from the pre-Revolution days are wont to call it – or in the frieze of cosy coffee shops clustered together in the Sayeh Tower opposite the Mellat Park. He's somewhat of a legend, venerated both abroad and at home: a reality that comes as a welcome surprise in a nation whose artists usually enjoy iconic status posthumously. I had spoken to him at length over the phone towards the end of his winter sojourn in Vancouver a few months earlier; he's certainly no stranger, although I've yet to meet him in person. The stifling heat is certainly not making the situation any more relaxing, and, as I finally manage to furl myself in the backseat of the tiny Peugeot, I feel a tepid patch of sweat underneath my arms. '*Agha*,' I say with diffidence, 'can you please turn on the cooler?' He casts a sidelong glance in the rearview mirror, flicks a switch, and we head for the dusty foothills of the Alborz Mountains.

As soon as we find our way onto the highway, we hit a gridlock. While the synth-soaked sounds of a maudlin pop song set to the proverbial 6/8 rhythm continue to emanate from the car radio and we find ourselves in a midday jam, the driver decides to while away the time by striking up conversation. 'What do you do?' he asks. Not having the patience to get into any details, I provide a desultory response. 'I'm in the arts.' 'Ah, are you a singer? A wedding singer?' comes the reply. *For God's sake, move!* I shout in vain in the recesses of my mind, looking ahead worriedly at the swarm of white and grey cars embellished with religious slogans and Zoroastrian icons. To add to the drama, the artist in question isn't picking up either of his telephones, and I wonder whether he'll be in his studio at all by the time we finally reach it.

At long last, our uphill journey comes to a welcome end in Niavaran – *almost*. The driver can't seem to find the artist's studio, and, exasperated by his continual circulations, I decide to call it a day and find it myself. Pulling the crumpled piece of paper out of the pocket of my cigarette jeans, I take a gamble and head down an unassuming side street. I still can't get a hold of the artist, and doubt whether any passersby or street sweepers can point me in the right direction. Just as I'm about to give up hope, I descry the tip of a metal statue jutting out above a battered metal door. *This must be it*, I think to myself. I hesitantly press the round, blackened buzzer, and, in a few moments, it clicks open. Standing before me is a silver *Heech* sculpture of massive proportions, which a flock of metalworkers is hurriedly trying to cover from an impending downpour.

Amidst the clamour, a man of average height with a mane of wavy white hair contrasting against his typically olive-hued Persian complexion, wearing a simple chequered shirt rolled up to his elbows and a pair of loose-fitting trousers, emerges from his studio. '*Salam*, Joobin', he says, warmly extending a soft yet roughened hand, before giving instructions to his artisans.

The monolith having been stowed away nicely, we all amble into his studio, where I'm greeted by two female apprentices and a host of assistants, one more welcoming than the next. After grabbing two wooden stools for himself and me, he calls upon one of those present for a box of Persian pastries and cups of steaming hot *chai*. For one with knowledge of Parviz Tanavoli's status as one of the most important and highest-grossing contemporary Iranian artists, it is difficult, to say the least, to match the man in the flesh with his grandiose reputation. Unlike the hipster artists who frequent the cafés, *baghs,* and galleries in Tehran's northern suburbs, many of whom are dead giveaways on account of their handlebar moustaches, pomegranate-inspired jewellery, and calligraphy-adorned headscarves and shawls (amongst other things), Tanavoli is the sort of person one could easily overlook on their way to the local bakery or corner store. 'Genuine' is the word that first comes to my mind as the humble, soft-spoken *ostad* and I begin chatting amiably about subjects ranging from the art 'scene' in Toronto and his current projects to my love affair with Iran and the influence of Persian culture on the Ottoman Turks.

* * *

As an artist, Tanavoli has often been compared to the mythical mason Farhad, whose labours on Mount Behistun and unrequited love for the Armenian princess Shirin were famously celebrated in Ferdowsi's *Shahnameh*, and later, Nezami's *Khosrow and Shirin*. The association couldn't be more appropriate. Their shared professions aside, the oeuvre of Tanavoli – an artist, scholar, collector, writer, and all-around Iranophile – has, particularly in the past decade, taken on a sort of mythical quality, and the mark he has made on Iranian art and culture throughout his illustrious and prolific career is sure to well outlive him in the annals of Iranian history and lore. Best known, perhaps, for his iconic *Heech* (*Nothingness*) series of sculptures, which have found their way into renowned museums, art galleries, and collections the world over, much of Tanavoli's art brings to the fore a dynamic interplay between traditional Iranian visual culture and modernist sensibilities.

Along with artists such as Hossein Zenderoudi, Marcos Grigorian, Faramarz Pilaram, and Sadegh Tabrizi, Tanavoli was one of the founders of the *Saqqa-Khaneh* (lit. 'Waterhouse') movement of contemporary Iranian art that flourished in the early sixties in Iran. Taking its name from the public drinking fountains found throughout Iran serving as a memory of the martyred Imam Hossein – whose army was deprived of water by the Caliph Yazid in the defining battle of Karbala – the *Saqqa-Khaneh* artists drew inspiration from the aesthetics and imagery featured in such sites, creating a form of 'spiritual' Iranian pop art in the process. In the case of Tanavoli, his childhood fascination with locks – prominent features in Iranian folk and Shi'a culture, often seen attached to the grilles of *saqqa-khanehs* and the tombs of saints – led him to pursue a career in sculpting, and become an artist many today consider the father of modern Iranian sculpture.

The aforesaid is not, however, to imply that Tanavoli is only looked at as a sculptor. In addition to his intricate and iconic sculptures, mostly cast in bronze, Tanavoli has produced countless paintings and mixed media works, and is the author of numerous books pertaining to visual Iranian culture, revolving around subjects such as tribal rugs, nomadic Iranian peoples, and, of course, locks. As well, a love for all things Iranian is something that shines in the artist's every endeavour; if I've ever seen a patriot, it's Tanavoli. Although usually reserved and collected whilst talking about his practice, he gets emotional speaking about Iran, and the fact that he has chosen to continue working there, despite his differences and incidents with the government, is indeed admirable. In talking with Tanavoli, I find him to be the personification of so many of the innumerable aspects of the complex Iranian spirit. Like the Bakthiaris, those noble Iranian tribesmen of old whose exploits were famously captured in the 1920s Hollywood film *Grass: A Nation's Battle for Life*, Tanavoli travels to and from his summer and winter 'pastures' in Tehran and Vancouver almost religiously. In addition to his nomadism, he lives with Persian poetry, that of Rumi in particular, and has always approached his art with the eyes and soul of a poet – a character whose words and deeds have held sway over the Iranian psyche since time immemorial. And, on a similar note, like medieval Iran's grand man of letters, Ferdowsi, who laboriously amassed the myths and legends of the ancient Iranians in his magnum opus, Tanavoli has always been somewhat of a scavenger, eagerly striving to collect, preserve, and reinterpret relics and artefacts pertaining to Iran's illustrious past. In a fairly recent publication of his, *Wonders of the Universe*, the artist describes how he stumbled upon the yellowed, inky Qajar-era lithographs of scenes from Sa'di's *Golestan* (*Rose Garden*) and Ghazvini's *Ajayeb ol Makhlughat va Gharayeb ol Mowjudat* (*The Wonders of Creation and Oddities of Existence*) – which he later adorned with swathes of pastel-hued gouache – whilst foraging through a heap of odds and sods in Tehran's weekly Friday Bazaar. Nomad, poet, Farhad of the age, preserver of tales fantastic and fabulous: these are only a few epithets that can attempt to translate the artist's legacy into words.

Of course, no discourse about the oeuvre of Parviz Tanavoli would be complete without mention of the artist's *Heech* series of sculptures, which have become inextricably linked to his name. To those unfamiliar with medieval Persian philosophy, the concept of *heech* may simply appear as a paradox or oxymoron; sculptures so grand, enveloping, and towering are presented as manifestations of nothingness. True, Tanavoli's concept of *heech* is certainly about nothingness, although this is nothingness in the grandest, most encompassing sense of the word. For the fatalist Omar Khayyam, this world was but a fleeting vision, a caravanserai on the path to oblivion – naught, which would fade into further nothingness. *Since save wind in our grasp,* *of what was remains naught,* he wrote, *since all that* *remains of what is, is brokenness and loss; it's as if all that* *isn't in this world is here – imagine that all that is in this* *world exists not*[1]. For the likes of Rumi and the Sufi poets, however, nothingness was more of a mystical concept; to them, like the authors of the *Upanishads,* the self (*nafs*) and the ego were mere illusions, drops of water in an ocean of truth – isolable to the eye of the uninitiated, yet indistinguishable to that of the mystic: to become nothing was to become *everything,* and vice-versa. It is, perhaps, more the latter Sufi interpretation that Tanavoli tries to capture in his sculptures than the philosophy of Khayyam, especially given his penchant for Rumi, although I can't help but notice traces of the Old Tent-Maker's influence in them as well. As hopeful and vivacious Tanavoli is as a person as well as an artist, I have sensed at times a sort of melancholy within him. His daunting throne-like monolith, *Oh Persepolis,* is perhaps a prime example of this. Wrought of solid brass and hacked in a script bearing a resemblance to Old Persian cuneiform, it stands as a sombre, evocative reminder of the lost glories of the Persian Empire, which at its peak stretched from the sunny shores of Greece to India. *Alas, for in vain* *did we waste away … With our desires unfulfilled, to* *oblivion we fell prey*[2], Khayyam might probably say with remorse, were he to behold Tanavoli's piece today. And Ferdowsi? *I spit on you, O wheel of the* *firmament! I spit on you!*

* * *

As Tanavoli jubilantly talks to me about the book he and his apprentices are working on – a three-dimensional *Book of Heech* – and takes me on a tour of his workshop, with its bits of scrap metal scattered about here and there, I begin likening the affable septuagenarian to a *naqqal*, a traditional Persian storyteller. Like the *gosans* of the Parthian era, the bards of today impassionedly recite epic tales and parables from the vast repository of Iranian lore, roving from stage to stage, coffeehouse to coffeehouse, as conduits of myth and magic. While he may not be a man of many words, he, like the fabled Farhad, is a poet and storyteller of form and beauty. Concealed within the artist's resplendent, undulating figures and images can be found not only pearls of Persian wisdom and universal truths, but also pages from tales of world-conquering kings, soul-conquering poets, rambling tribesmen, and tragic heroes. Verily do they tell, with eloquence and artistry, the story of the land of Iran.

Outside, in breezy Niavaran, the swarthy sky is pregnant with foreboding. As I bid the *ostad* farewell, nurturing hope within my breast that we will meet again soon, my phone begins buzzing in my pocket. 'So, how was your meeting? What did you talk about for so long?' asks my friend. 'Nothing. And everything. And nothing', I say, as I

try to find a ride back to the winding alleys of
Zafar.

1/12/2015

Bibliography

1. Bekhrad, J. *The Quatrains of Omar Khayyam.*
   Bloomington: Balboa Press, 2017.
2. Ibid.

The First Time Ever I Saw Your Face

Familiar stranger, I love thee;
To the land of tales, take me …

I can remember it vividly: the aroma of a hot pot of *fesenjoon* was seeping forth from the kitchen, while I gazed at the patterns of the Persian carpet beneath my knees, tracing familiar shapes with my finger and sipping on bitter, hot tea that traced its way down my tiny throat. In the background, my parents and relatives were bandying alien words about politics, work, and the state of things in the motherland. I couldn't have cared less, though; the little characters and shapes before me – which seemed like figures from a fantasy novel – in my indoor substitute for cloud-gazing were far more interesting. Besides, I couldn't understand half of the things they were saying; I was a *bisavad* little *bacheh* who found solace in his daydreams, terrified of what the next school day would bring.

As I was losing myself in the twists and turns on the floor, a rainbow burst forth from the television screen, demanding the attention of one and all. The notes warbled, the picture was fuzzy, and it all seemed like the stuff of an afternoon children's programme; yet, that moment so fixed itself in my memory that I'll forever associate it with the shorthaired woman driving the red automobile behind a green screen. '*Ee, Googoosh-e!*' I heard my mother exclaim behind me, as my eyes glued themselves to the TV. I didn't know who this woman in the funny little car was, but I felt like I knew her; she looked a bit like my Persian teacher, I thought, and I surmised she could have been one of the endless number of cousins my parents kept telling me I had back in Iran. I didn't dwell on things too much, though; I just knew I liked the pretty lady who sang nice songs about birds and drove a cute car.

* * *

Throughout my childhood, Googoosh continued to surface intermittently. Sometimes, while bored on lazy Sunday afternoons, when no friends were around on the block to play with, I'd go rummaging through the nooks and crannies of our house in suburban Toronto looking for treasure. Going through my parents' cassette collection, I'd often find, amongst Gipsy Kings and Strunz & Farah tapes, some by Googoosh. Although nobody I asked knew Googoosh's last name, I thought I'd finally discovered it when I came across a yellowed cover with jumbled letters that looked like the black ones on the façades of old cinemas. This time, Googoosh looked like my mother; I could see her more clearly, her dark Persian eyes, rouge lipstick, and characteristically Iranian gaze resembling something halfway between disgust and languor. *So that's her last name*, I thought to myself: *Mahpishooni*! I didn't know what 'Mahpishooni' meant, but it sounded alluring and plausible as a Persian last name. After being processed through the mind of an eight-year-old child, however, it transformed into 'Mafishoni'. Mrs Googoosh Mafishoni's newest fan was a kid on a sleepy street in Thornhill.

Although Googoosh wasn't the only pre-Revolution pop star featured on my relatives' televisions and radios, I always felt, somewhat instinctively, that she was in a class of her own. Ebi looked like the sort of person I'd see in a *chelo kababi* restaurant, and was apparently quite the drinker; as such, in my child's mind, I saw him as an addict, a *very* bad man. Only in my twenties would I rediscover him as the epitome of rock and roll; and, as my father could never stand Dariush (and still can't), I crossed him off my list as well. With *sonnati* music seeming to my ears like melancholia from another planet, it only left Googoosh, whom I came to identify with Persian music altogether. Everybody loved Googoosh, and, as a child, she became something of a maternal figure to me, a woman to revere and idolise. Even in my teens, I hadn't heard most of her songs, and couldn't, like some of my other Iranian friends, recite verses of her tunes by heart; but I still loved her – albeit in a very different way than I loved the Stones.

As a child and teenager, Googoosh represented my mysterious homeland, the golden days of the

Joobin Bekhrad

Pahlavis my grandparents and parents would often speak about with tears in their eyes, and the beauty of the Persian language and culture. In my first year of university, however, as I fell in love with my heritage and strove to escape the monotony and vapidity of business school, I rediscovered Googoosh. As part of my quest to find myself and absorb everything and anything having to do with Iran, Googoosh became a guide of sorts. In the car, on my way to and from university on the endless expanse of the highway, Googoosh was my Persian instructor, teaching me new flowery words and helping me improve what my grandfather called my 'Armenian' accent. She also provided the soundtrack to my readings about pre and post-Revolution Iran, making me nostalgic for a time I'd never experienced, and inciting a yearning for fabled halcyon days long gone. I bought a collection of her old music videos from Pars Video, which I watched over and over again with relish, ditching rock riffs to instead learn the mellifluous chord changes to *Man Amadeh-am* (*I Have Come*) and *Marham* (*Balm*). I wished I could have been there with my father and uncle when they took a picture with her in Abadan as kids, seen her and Behrouz Vossoughi in *Mah-e Asal* (*Honeymoon*) on a summer evening amidst the smell of sausage sandwiches and sunflower seeds, and rubbed shoulders with Tehrani teenagers when she sang *Digeh Geryeh Del-o Va Nemikoneh* (*Crying Won't Console Me Anymore*) for the first time at the Koochini club. As this sweet-singing shape-shifter assumed in fuzzy footage the look of mother, my Armenian math teacher from high-school, Farah Fawcett, and an epicene (Bowie, eat your heart out), she brought me nearer to a past and history so close, and yet so far away. Memories of a previous life were awakened; I'd been there all along, and, through Googoosh, the past came rushing forth in vivid colour.

* * *

'There was wine, tears, and the sound of Googoosh', a Yemeni friend once told me, describing a Saturday evening in New York City. *What connection to Googoosh could a twenty-something Yemeni have?* I thought. *How can an icon belonging to my parents' generation still inspire Iranians and non-Iranians alike, young and old?* Ramesh may have been funkier, and Hayedeh more technically accomplished, but it's been Googoosh *Khanum* upon whose head has rested the crown of popular Iranian music – and culture – for decades, despite a period of obscurity in the years following the Revolution. Hers is the voice of a displaced generation, of turbulent, heady, and happy times that burned away as fast as they came into being; a voice that has remained impassioned and undaunted through decades dark and dolorous, a glimmer of hope for the future, a reminder of hidden beauty and splendour. Cyrus is the Father, and Googoosh the Daughter, if there's ever been one.

Joobin Bekhrad

'There's the air you breathe, the water you drink, the food you eat, and the Rolling Stones', Keith Richards once said, remarking on his band's longevity. 'And Googoosh', I would have added. For all her fame and prominence, however, Googoosh's voice will not bring to my mind any of the rather grandiose statements and remarks I've just made, but rather that pretty shorthaired lady in the funny automobile of simpler, innocent days.

8/17/2015

Yashar, My Hero

> ... Beyond this smooth plowed land the
> scrub of the Chukurova begins. Thickly
> covered with a tangle of brushwood, reeds,
> blackberry brambles, wild vines, and
> rushes, its deep green expanse seems
> boundless, wilder and darker than a forest
> ...[1]

Those were some of the first lines of Yashar
Kemal's I ever read, and I knew, somewhat
instinctively, that they would be far from the last. I
wasn't a Turkish schoolboy trudging through *de
rigeur* reading, but rather a bored, daydreaming
university student in Toronto caught between the
dead of winter and the doldrums of a third
semester. I had recently devoured a dog-eared
English translation of *The Book of Dede Korkut* –
which I'd gotten my hands on with not little
difficulty – and was ravenous for more tales about
minstrels, bandits, chivalry, and the steppe.
Together with my obscure Persian romances and
folk tales, Caucasian legends, Zoroastrian texts,
and desert travelogues, I had wrought a haven of
sorts for myself in humdrum suburbia. Before one
book was finished, I'd be eagerly seeking out the
next; I never wanted to leave that fantastic realm,
to come back down from the clouds to a less-than-
romantic reality. Come to think of it, I never have,
really. Little did I know that one bleak, snowy

February's day, right before three agonising hours of prattle to be washed down with bland black coffee, I'd be given the keys not to that magical realm, but a universe unto itself. With great expectations and the fervour of a famished waif, I tore open a little brown parcel I found waiting for me in the icy mailbox at the end of my street and extended a hand to wise old Mr Kemal, who took me down to the burning fields of the thistle-strewn Chukurova …

* * *

I've never had many heroes in life that breathed; most of them have long discarded their earthly corpuses, and their visages are at best the product of artistic interpretation. For life lessons and to learn about the ways of the world, I've looked to Omar Khayyam, and for the blueprint for the Iranian I've always aspired to be, Cyrus the Great. To write, read, dream, and love, I've always taken my cues from Mr Kemal. As I sit writing this eulogy, I'm overlooked by scores of his books on my shelf. Each one corresponds to a particular episode in my life I can vividly recall, and collectively, line by line and word by word, they've come to profoundly influence not only my approach towards writing, but also my worldview, my philosophies, and my entire being.

It all began on that wintry afternoon with *Memed, My Hawk,* the first novel in the *Ince Memed* tetralogy, and perhaps Yashar Kemal's best-known work. When it comes to novels, I'm notoriously difficult to please. I've divided my collection into two categories: ones I still remember, and those I'll probably forget I ever owned five years down the line. Needless to say, Kemal's proudly inhabit the top shelves of the former. When I read the first lines of *Memed*, the first thing that struck me was not only the beauty of Kemal's descriptions, but also the lyrical air of his writing. From cover to cover, it read like poetry, and I've always been as much indebted to Kemal as I have to his late wife, Thilda, who with beauty and uncanny precision, translated all the English editions of his novels. I identified with Memed, that skinny village boy, shared in his trials and triumphs, and wanted to ride with him until the end – the end of the Chukurova, the end of the plains of southern Turkey by the Mediterranean, the end of time itself. Memed's origins were a mystery, and I often fancied that he might have, like Mr Kemal himself, been a Kurd; that would have made us kin. And who better to have as kin than the hero of the oppressed, the king of bandits, the saviour of the steppe, Slim Memed?

Through Memed – as well as the myriad other characters that populated his novels – Kemal gave a voice to a people on the margins of society, alone and without agency both at home, as well as abroad. Like the sublime R.K. Narayan, who with brilliance moulded the world of Malgudi that provided the setting to all his novels, almost all of Yashar Kemal's works were situated in either the Chukurova, or at least rural Anatolia. However, unlike Narayan's fictional Malgudi, the Chukurova was an actual place. Kemal himself was born and raised there, a fact that found its way onto the dust jacket of every one of his books. The Chukurova of Kemal's pages was a sultry, bewitching land brimming with Turks, Kurds, Armenians, Circassians, and other neighbouring peoples, who, although they found themselves as part of a progressive and 'modern' Turkish Republic in 1923 (courtesy of the 'blue-eyed devil', as one Kemal called the other, through a character), still very much belonged to the past. Airplanes would occasionally fly over the fields, and *beys* drive into villages in slick black Benzes, but Kemal's characters were barely literate, if at all, and knew little about life outside the village. Of what concern was the world beyond to them when there was fresh cotton to be picked, debts to be repaid, *ağas* to be appeased, and survival to be fought for with outstretched hands?

For subject matter, Kemal didn't have to look too far; the Chukurova was a subject in itself. Through honeyed prose and bewildering simplicity, Kemal described to me the plight of villagers as they picked bolls of cotton under the beating sun, and how they'd later drink *raki* and dance the *halay;* the lay of lovers within thickets of grass, far from watching eyes; the passion and fear of thrusting a rusty blade through the back of a cruel *muhtar*; and the cry of a minstrel recounting heroic exploits with a *saz*. And all without the slightest trace of artifice. You could tell Kemal had been through everything; this was stuff you simply couldn't make up. Kemal knew the taste and feel of the black Chukurova soil and the wind from the Taurus Mountains, and the smell of burning thistles. He had made fresh *yufka* bread with his bare hands, the same ones he had used to pick cotton. He'd seen his adopted brother stab his father to death, and lost an eye in the same incident. He was the Chukurova personified: a living, breathing repository of tales, traditions, rituals, myths, legends, and magic – and I felt it in my bones.

As with any prolific author, there were certain elements that characterised Kemal's writing, and which, in a sense, served as his 'signature'. Kemal, unlike Orhan Pamuk – upon whom Kemal's longstanding title of 'Turkey's greatest living author' was seemingly conferred by international critics – grew up far away from the hubbub and clamour of Istanbul in southern Turkey, and it was only with great difficulty that he was able to attend university in the big city; and, in contrast to Pamuk, Kemal was of a people whose very existence was denied by the Turkish Republic, simply dismissed as 'mountain Turks'. In an ethnic sense, as well as from the perspective of social status, Kemal was born and raised on the fringe (even his wife, Thilda, wasn't an ethnic Turk, but a

Jew), and therefore it should come as no surprise
that the bulk of his novels championed the
underdog. From the legendary Slim Memed, a sort
of modern Koroğlu figure who rebelled against the
oppressive Abdi *Ağa*, to tiny Memidik who
dreamed of killing the dastardly *Muhtar* Sefer in
the *Wind from the Plain* trilogy, and Halil Zalimoğlu,
who finally burned down his *ağa*'s house in *Salman
the Solitary*, the downtrodden were often the focus of
Kemal's literature.

His books are also marked by his vivid, lengthy
descriptions of the seemingly ordinary, to which he
would impart a tinge of magic. By the end of one
of his novels, I'd know every nook and cranny of
the Anavarza crags, and enjoy a whole new
vocabulary pertaining to flora and fauna. In the
middle of a scene, Kemal would stop to explain, in
lucid prose, to his dear reader the way a particular
flower blossomed, the difference between cotton
collected before and after a downpour, the process
of baking bread, the slope of a mountain. For
some, such details may seem as unnecessary asides
that only serve to lengthen a literary work; for me,
they were the very essence of Kemal's writing, the
raison d'être of his books. One could even go so far
as to say that everything else – plot, character, and
the like – came afterwards.

Where character was concerned, perhaps Kemal's
most profound contribution was the way in which
he highlighted the power – and danger – of myths,

and the role they played in his culture. Life was difficult in Kemal's Anatolia; simply surviving was the ultimate trial. As such, his characters needed and thrived on hope, seeking it wherever they could. In the process, a skinny village lad, after a few deeds, was transformed through hearsay into a brazen hero of epic proportions, and a simple villager into a saint who would not be referred to as *Uncle* Tashbash, but rather *Our Lord* Tashbash, he amongst the ranks of the Forty Holy Men. The transformations were preposterous, ridiculous, and comical, even – but they were also incredibly plausible. Kemal's characters believed in the heroes and monsters they themselves created; they feared them, worshipped them, would die for them, and killed for them. These days, I often wonder what's being said about Kemal in the Turkish media. I haven't read any obituaries yet; his work, and the experiences I've had with it, have made me more familiar with the man than any article ever will. It would indeed be ironic if Kemal were to turn into the very sort of hero he so feared in his writings. 'He wrote in his mother's womb', one might be saying now; 'He traded one eye for a magic pen'; 'He was seen the other night in the Chukurova, a halo of fire blazing about his countenance ...'

And, of course, there was Kemal's writing style. Never was there an unnecessary sentence, nor was a word ever heedlessly tossed into his cauldron. Passages were terse where they needed to be, and drawn out as necessary. True, Kemal often sent me running to my dictionary; but it was never to look up some obfuscating, obsolete term that had only wriggled its way into academic exegeses. Reading Kemal was an education in every aspect, and I was only too happy to sink my hands into the warm earth of the Chukurova and rise with handfuls of flowery words. If you ask me who my influences are with respect to the guitar, I'll be quick to answer: Keith Richards, Mick Taylor, Chuck Berry, Johnny Thunders. On the contrary, I've never really thought about my literary influences. Hanif Kureishi's early characters fascinated me, and Iraj Pezeshkzad's ability to take a snapshot of an era and an entire culture and transform that into a novel continues to astound me. Where actual *writing* is concerned, however, I've always looked to Mr Kemal. Prose writing is often considered passé these days, with many readers and novelists instead fixated on driving plots, unexpected twists, and attention-grabbing elements. Sentences have become shorter and vocabularies simplified, and 'conventions' are being ditched in favour of 'modern' approaches to writing. Like his own characters, Kemal was from a world of ages past – a reality that well manifested itself in his writing. He was a romantic, a dreamer, a poet, and, above all, a storyteller. To tell the tale of the Chukurova, Kemal chose to do so in the way he knew best, and maybe the only way that would ever really do: as a spellbound bard.

Whenever reading Kemal's books, I always had the feeling that he was the last of his kind. No authors today speak to me as he did, as writers like R.K. Narayan did. They write stories, but aren't storytellers. They win prizes, but don't move me. Their careers are based on a quest for the next compelling subject, the next idea, the next character. People have often told me that many of my pieces don't have clear beginnings or ends; I take it as a compliment. I've always looked up to giants like Kemal, for whom the 'destination' was never the issue at hand; the *feelings* were, the emotions, the ambience, the experience. Novels necessitate plots, but writers like Kemal showed they didn't have to be complicated, or even the focus of a work. Yashar Kemal reminded me of the beauty – and importance – of language and storytelling, and the significance of authenticity. I'll never write a novel about an Anatolian or Iranian village, because I've never lived in one; and if I ever do visit one, the most I can hope for is a superficial experience. Kemal taught me that you can best write about what you *know.* Sure, I could always write about unfamiliar subjects, and what I write might even be well-received; but it would never be half as good. And by good, I mean *real.*

* * *

A week ago, I was in my Toronto apartment finishing the last lines of *The Undying Grass,* the final installment in the *Wind from the Plain* trilogy. I don't know why I'd put off reading the book for so long. Our Lord Tashbash had finally passed away, Memidik had done away with *Muhtar* Sefer for good, and the proud eagle, once humiliated by the village children, soared above the Chukurova cotton fields with outstretched wings:

> The great eagle was flying off towards the distant mountains. Three times he wheeled round and round at the far end of the Chukurova land. Then he glided off towards Mount Aladağ.[2]

That is, perhaps, how I'll always remember Mr Kemal – as a proud, resilient bird flying high above the blessed Chukuorva. When I closed the book, I caressed its cover with my cracked, dry hands, and kissed it, as I often do with books that have touched me. The next morning, shortly after I awoke, I read the news to find out Mr Kemal had passed away the previous day. Our story ended just as it began – on a cold, mid-winter's day in February – only I wasn't a lost and bored university student, but a boy transformed.

Thank you, Mr Kemal, for the stories and the magic that will live on in me forever.

3/9/2015

In memory of Yashar Kemal (1923 – 2015).

Bibliography

1. Kemal, Y. *Memed, My Hawk.* New York City: New York Review Books Classics, 2005.
2. Kemal, Y. *The Undying Grass.* London: Collins & Harvill Press, 1977.

Joobin Bekhrad

I Want to Cry Like Soraya

I really should be getting on, but I don't want to go to the gathering; no, anything but that. The sun is again but a memory, this chichi avenue draped in damning black and blue; whoever said autumn was romantic can go to hell. Behind those hissing maws of steel, a pale-faced boy is licking coffee grounds from his thumb whilst half-heartedly listening to the eschatological banter of a bundled-up blonde. Could this vignette be any more miserable? I suppose things can always get worse; I mean, just imagine if Phil Collins were to pop on the radio. Maybe it's just the weather and the grim reality of November, and I shouldn't think too much about things. I've heard it's been snowing quite a bit in Tehran. It's difficult to imagine, because I've never seen Tehran at this time of year. Like the sun, it seems so far away; but then again, it would, even if I were tossed in the smoggy thick of the city. I always seem to have my head in the clouds and stars in my eyes, but I wouldn't have it any other way. Yes, I am a year older, and yes, if I don't make a move, the gods will take a proper piss on me, but – I wonder what the streets of Tehran look like now …

* * *

They must be lying under sullied shrouds of snow, the boughs blanketing endless Vali-ye Asr Avenue, the skirt of the Alborz Mountains. I don't know why, out of all the times I found myself glued to the backseat of a *Paykan* careening hell for leather towards the idyll of Darband, I never once bothered to venture past the creaky gates of the Zahir-o'Dowleh cemetery. But what would have been the point? It is not in his strange, beloved homeland that Sadegh lies, but faraway Paris, cold and grey. Beside his pointed gravestone in Père Lachaise, Grandpa read the *fateheh* and made poor Sadegh roll over. At the very least, he'd escaped the clutches of the dreaded undertakers, in whose hands he would have 'died twice'[1].

What had taken Sadegh to Paris and wrested him from the Iran he so loved, but which could never love him back? Dashed dreams and a heavy heart, just like Sa'edi, a stone's throw away from Sadegh, just like Soraya. Sadegh's undoing was that he knew too much. He'd read the story of Iran, and over its bloodied pages wept in vain; and, in searching for Iran, he found himself on the torrid shores of Hindustan, to which his people were bound in blood and spirit alike. No sooner did he catch sight of a twinkling of hope, though, than Sol couched behind that humbled lion and his chimeras crumbled to dust. But unlike Sae'di, who in lieu of the liberties he so sought found Parisian exile and a bottle, Sadegh perhaps fared better. Having failed to drown himself in the River Marne, Sadegh finally found freedom from the fetters of his cruel reality lying supine on his pillow, as if lost in a child's dream, in his gassed flat on Rue Championnet. Iran had lost a lover once and for all, but outside, it was just another uneventful April's day in Paris.

As Sadegh before her had carried the burden of knowledge with him to his frigid grave, Soraya did that of her pride; Sadegh *knew* too much, and Soraya *wanted* too much. She wouldn't play second fiddle to anyone, neither in this life nor the next. It may have mattered little to the King of Kings and the girl with the mousy hair, but not to the *Principessa*, to whom certain things were holy, inviolable. *You could have had it all!* Yes, your Imperial Highness, you could have faded away, slowly, watching your soul splinter into a thousand little pieces in those glittering glass halls, day in, day out. They would have wrapped you, an afterthought, in velvet and mink, and sent you to live out the rest of your days in the shadow of what you once used to be; and you, feigning joy, would smile and wave a bejewelled hand, comforted beneath satin sheets only by the thought that you were a 'queen'. But what need had you for petty titles when you would always be a queen, with or without God's Shadow? You would have rather died than sully that which you deemed sacred, and, above all, submit – just like Sadegh, just like Sa'edi. Three faces, three souls, each with the same desire, all of which met their untimely ends broken and alone in the city of lights.

* * *

Sombre nymph of fire and stardust, the ring of clinking sheep bells in your ears and flowers smeared upon your visage; as you beheld your splendour then, you recalled Egypt's fallen daughter and fair Lilith. Even the thought of them, though, was not enough to dull the glow of your eyes, daubed with brightest white. Fawzia's story you knew all too well, and in Lilith you saw sororal kin; Lilith, banished from the Garden for not succumbing to Adam's whims. *Cursed she may be,* you thought, caressing your powdered cheeks, *but she still has her pride.* Eve roamed then about Paradise, bearing upon her head a wreath not of leaves, but of jewels, bone, and Aryan light. *So be it*: you knew their time in Paradise, unlike your beauty, would come to pass; the house would fall, the Garden become but a haunting thought.

So much for Lilith. What became of our *Principessa*? Far from the Marble Palace, she gave up the ghost in her 'Palace of Loneliness' fifteen years ago, down and out in Paris: just like Sadegh, just like Sa'edi. Would that they in their misery, had, like Michaux, found a miracle; but alas, there are none to be found in exile's bleak hollow. Lady Stardust lives now amongst the stars, as does the lad who fell from up above; and Eve now weeps not for them, but Leila, Leila, Leila, whom they finally took away. Clinking glasses with ghosts and misty-eyed sycophants, Persia's favoured child remembers the paradise lost with heavy sighs in Paris.

* * *

And here I am in Toronto, beneath the incandescent bulbs of some wretched little café, turning my eyes away from the night sky. Mithras will come soon, that bringer of light, to herald the dawn and the end of our suffering; that I know. But for now, there's only darkness, the nothingness of November, and the creeping death of winter. If only I could be like you, Soraya. I don't want to be like common people and cry like they do; I don't want to cry over cold Americanos in my torn blue jeans. I want to cry like you, *Principessa*. I want to cry like Soraya. For what, though? My tears wouldn't change anything, or bring you back. What could they ever do? '*Dir shodeh, joonam*', I can hear you saying, swallowing the bitterness of it all. 'It's too late, my dear …'

11/29/2016

In memory of Soraya Esfandiary Bakhtiari (1932 – 2001), Sadegh Hedayat (1903 – 1951), and Gholam-Hossein Sa'edi (1936 – 1985).

Bibliography

1. Hedayat, S. *Three Drops of Blood*. Richmond: Alma Books, 2012.

Learning Hindi in Paris
An Evening with Hindi Zahra

Sidelong glances, dumbfounding back alleys, madcap laughs, and piss-soaked holes in the ground; Paris, how I love thee. I should be so lucky: not so long ago you had my brethren on their knees, they who succumbed to a heady perfume, whose scent seemed to rise ever upwards, a beacon amidst the benighted signalling progress, power – *modernité!* From pied *divans* they looked to you, westwards, for succour and stimuli, lost in a fog of sweet opium smoke, their heads reeling with thick purple elixir and the smell of roses. To them, down and out in smoky Teheran, you were the pearl of the West; your children were fair and wore flowers in their hair, as once said a bopping imp. They sipped on bubbly, read *belles lettres* in their pleasure gardens, sat on four legs, and prodded their grub with strange metallic things. These, you see, were the trappings of civilised men, *de rigeur* for those of taste and worth, the stuff of substance for the backwards (albeit handsome) brute wishing to ingratiate himself amongst the new conquerors of the world.

And so it transpired that one bittersweet Tuesday afternoon, the rain having soaked the grey blotches of cobblestone outside my window, I found myself – a Persian abroad – in the sordid lap of Madame Paris, looking for a decent bite to eat. After doing up the laces of a shiny pair of soft leather shoes that made me blush with all their clicking and clacking, I made my way downstairs to amble about the *passages* encircling my hotel in Saint-Georges, just close enough as to be able to retrace my steps. I've never been that much of a gourmand, and it's easy to get distracted in that city; any thoughts I had of 1664 (that most glorious of years) and the effluvia of local cheese were fast allayed. In a store window, I espied Mughal-style dressers, chintz curtains, and sequinned slippers; further up the street, a French-pressed Stones vinyl stopped me in my tracks, and I soon lost track of time altogether when I stumbled onto a picturesque side street dotted with little guitar shops. The selections were rather odd, and I spotted, lying demurely amongst the blackies and butterscotch blondes, the guitar my mother once (very briefly) strummed on as a child: a red and white Danelectro, lined with bright faux snakeskin. I can never help but stop and stare at these things – I, who have only ever wanted to live on water and feed on lightning. Just like Johnny.

* * *

Her voice had come to me, in splotches of colour and clouds of powder, on the smooth wings of a Saharan breeze during the cool, wet days of an otherwise uneventful April. She looked rather odd, staring at me boyishly in a candy store of sorts, at once exuding the aura of a Riffian ruffian and the emaciated Keef wannabe from Manhattan. Filthy humbuckers, rusty strings of steel, and the roughened tongue of the mountains got me pricking up my ears again in exultation. Punk is not dead, and rock keeps rolling; these amorphous phenomena simply shape-shift with the times, shaking all over all the while. She hath the fury of Eberhardt, the swagger of Choukri, the grit of the Cheikha; her head ain't green, and her hands ain't blue: she's a white-hot woman, through and through – and boy, can this skinny pretty thing *howl*. Little did I know then that my journey to discover the hallowed place where, as she had once told me, the skin speaks secret words in Spanish, would one day lead me to a grungy hovel on Rue Notre Dame de Lorette.

* * *

I did it again: I quaffed far too much of the red stuff. I should have known better. A wino I am, though one with his wits (usually) about him; so what was I doing, sipping to surfeit? Blame it on the sun – or, perhaps, the perverse effect of that sprawling den of iniquity. Though in Paris, I was indifferent to my surroundings, and could only think of faraway lands: Esfahan, Tangier, whitewashed Algiers. In my tattered tote, torn and frayed, Wharton's *In Morocco* jostled against a dog-eared copy of Chardin's *Voyage en Perse* I was reading again, for God knows what reason. They both made rather entertaining travel companions,

Joobin Bekhrad

Wharton and Chardin, the one with her bigotry and casual racism, and the other with his vignettes of fair Persia, as seen through the eyes of a fluffy-haired French jeweller. I lay my embroidered rug bookmark on a yellowed page, having finished a passage by Chardin that provided a fitting denouement to that lazy afternoon:

> The Courtiers, Gentlemen, and Rakes, drink Wine, and as they all use it, as a Remedy against Sorrow, and that one Part drink it to put them to Sleep, and the other to warm and make them Merry; they generally drink the Strongest, and most Heady, and if this does not make them presently Drunk, they say 'what Wine is this?'[1]

* * *

'*Quoi?*' asked a porter outside a nearby hotel. So much for all those wasted childhood years of learning French; I'd have been better off sticking to English. 'Where is Barbès?' He mumbled something incoherent to my virgin ears, and waved his sunburned hands about to guide me. I didn't see the infernal Tower, or go sauntering down the Champs, but I did go for a most pleasant stroll on Rue Barbès, the street where French propriety goes to die. 'Zey aghh not considéghhed *cool*, ze peepel in Baghhbès', a Moroccan friend of mine had told me over a pint the previous evening. 'Zey aghh not

– how you say – integghhating wit ze *société*.' Well, they were certainly a cool bunch of cats to me; ever since I saw a spunky young Rachid Taha laud the niceties of the boulevard, sandwiched between two portly, dolled-up broads, I'd wanted to visit the place. *We've got no problems … in Barbès! The world is beautiful … in Barbès!* Who wouldn't want to go there? It wasn't my idea, though; Happy and the girl called Gainsbourg wanted to down some lager and popcorn in a side street brasserie, before our time as pupils.

Tender was the night: it smelled of sex, sweat, and cigarettes. Happy, whilst waiting in the zigzagging queue, popped in quickly to a nearby souvenir shop to buy a magnet with a picture of a black cat on it, while I cringed at the viscose shawls patterned with Persian pickles beneath a set of hot fluorescent lights. Inside the theatre, all rococo and crushed velvet, the bastard beer took its toll, all of us scrambling to let loose in the loos. We emerged to find the darkened place brimming with bohemians in blue jeans, who had taken just about every half-decent seat left. We didn't want to disband, and, damn it, I hadn't ventured across the miserable English Channel to groove to the sight of a pillar. *Stand up on your two feet, baby – that's how it's got to be.* She would have wanted it that way, perhaps, and the various toxins I'd ingested throughout the day had, in any case, inured me to most forms of minor discomfort. One night is not, after all, a thousand, as is said in Persian; but O, would that it could be.

Unbeknownst to us, a renegade mariachi band had hooked up with a brigand on the *gumbri* and blind bluesmen from the Mississippi, and hit the high road for the 'Kesh. Smoke swirled about in ringlets amidst the glowing apertures, and you, the lanky girl with raven hair, emerged from the shadows to a fanfare of corroded nickel, greasy trumpets, and stinging overdrive. Your feet tapping, slender bejewelled hands clutching golden rays, hips swaying, teeth a'gnashin', my eyes beheld Frida and my ears heard Billie. I can't figure you out, put my finger on you, svelte songstress from the land of faded blue tattoos and leering *djinns*. Whence came that bewitching melody? Andalusia melted into a shotgun shack in Mississippi, shamans made wild love to witch doctors on the steppe, and a voodoo priest danced with a dervish in the glow of the moonlight, on curls of hashish. You taught us, the uninitiated, how to dance, how to *roll*; there, in the frenzied throng, in the squalor of the Cigale, we were given a lesson in Hindi. The girl beside me shut her eyes, tuned in, and dropped out, waving her long arms gently and pressing herself every now and again against the shiny black balustrades behind her. We were wet, hot, and strung out on cheap thrills, riding waves of raw electric euphoria, watching you writhe about in a halo of light, shaking violently and tossing your swarthy black locks, spellbound. Dancing girls, their anklets and castanets tinkling amidst the clamour flitted by in the darkness, silver revolvers let fly a hail of bullets, and Baba Zar laughed all the while, confabulating with spirits malevolent and benign in furtive, husky whispers.

* * *

Gainsbourg clutched my bony hand in hers as we pushed our way through the damp horde, making for the dirty avenue outside. The world turned azure, and amidst boozy banter and the ruffling of denim, you were there, alone, bidding the night farewell. The once-teeming theatre was pouring itself out onto the back alleys of Pigalle, and under a bright, burning bulb, you sang a song – not of darkness and disgrace – but of strange, ephemeral beauty. Gainsbourg's grasp tightened, and I was slowly led away, reluctantly, watching you recede into that from which you had emerged.

Not a word was said as we three, guided by stars and street lamps, sought Guimard's letters and a good time in the silence of a brisk, black night that would soon disappear in sweet billows.

6/22/2015

Bibliography

1. Chardin, Sir J. *Travels in Persia 1673 – 1677.* Mineola: Dover, 1988.

Joobin Bekhrad

The House of Sassan

I don't know why I chose to wear snakeskin-print slippers that day, but I did. London was burning, and Nice, as the heavens would have it, wasn't any cooler. As much as the sweat on my back was soaking through my shirt, I tried, with my dream-fazed eyes, to soak up the landscape. I hadn't been to Nice before, and, sitting in the backseat of the taxi, fancied myself a hotshot reporter on my way to Cannes; all I needed was a tweed jacket. My eyes flickered back and forth between the idyllic scenery and the meter, which was escalating faster than we were ascending the winding mountains. I bit the back of my hot sweaty hand, and fingered around in the pockets of my skinny blue jeans for cash. *Would it have killed you to get a few more Euros?* I thought to myself. *Step on it, mate!* I hadn't the slightest clue where we were going, and had only a vague idea of the man I was about to meet; but that's what summers are for, aren't they? To throw the refuge of winter to the wind, to feel, if but for a moment, like a wide-eyed child again, with the sun boring through your breast.

We passed by glistening bodies in faded polo shirts, while the world below dissolved into a brilliant sheet of blue. Highgate and Hampstead seemed further away than ever then; and, after the meter hit a perfectly round fifty and I ambled out before a towering cream-coloured villa, I remembered the time I'd gotten lost in some industrial wasteland in Dubai just a few months before. *What if this isn't the place?* I wondered, just as I heard a voice from above and espied a tuft of dirty blonde locks. *So you're this Sassan I keep hearing about, huh? Let's see what you've got.*

The door automatically opened, and not even the massive stone lions that greeted me were enough to wrest from me the confidence that my little snakeskin-print slippers afforded me that afternoon. *Nah, he doesn't look even half as cool as me …*

* * *

Perhaps the swanky northern suburbs of Tehran would have made for a more apt setting; but, for now, Saint-Jean-Cap-Ferrat – just a stone's throw away from Monaco – is where the man who signs with the initials B.B. calls home. Sassan Behnam Bakhtiar's art brought us together, initially, but we soon connected on a much deeper level (French wine, of course, played no small role in this). A few months prior to our meeting, a piece of mine had appeared right before a feature on him in a well-known magazine, whose editor had happened to conflate our names. He knew I was mad about all things Iranian, and his art – with its abundance of Iranian motifs, ancient and traditional – didn't fail to catch my eye. He wanted to know more about the skinny kid in London banging on about Iran, and I, about the Iranophile artist I'd heard some

Joobin Bekhrad

call a 'man on a mission' living it up in the south of France. If it was art that first ignited a connection, a love of Iran kept the spark alight.

Like my writing, Sassan's work revolves around Iran: he writes poems about Iranian villages. He looks at Achaemenid soldiers as his brothers. He reveres the spirit of his nomadic Bakhtiari ancestors. In short, he lives and breathes Iran. But how, some may ask, did this strapping, young thirty-something man, born in Paris and now residing near Monaco, come to devote his life and work to the culture of a country so often slighted – or, at best, ignored – in the West? And, of what stuff, exactly, is the 'Iran' consuming his every thought? I've always said that there are many ideas of Iran, each one a reality in its own right. Iran means different things to Iranians, and Sassan isn't one to put forth his particular vision in subtle terms. He often says that he strives to show his audiences the 'real' Iran – that is, an ancient, glorious land, as culturally rich and influential as it was millennia ago as it is today. Take it or leave it. 'Whoever wants to join me can join me. I'm not asking for acceptance.'

The foundations of the House of Sassan – to make a connection to the celebrated dynasty known, amongst other things, for having brought proud Rome to its knees on more than one occasion – were laid thirty-odd years ago in Paris. On the little metropolitan island of Ile Saint-Louis, Sassan grew up with his father, who first introduced him to painting and instilled in him a love of expression through the arts. The young artist was a Parisian, born and bred, until the age of ten, when his mother decided to take him and his brother to Tehran. The move was a life-changing one, not unlike my first visit to Iran as a teenager. 'Before, I was just a typical French kid', he said, twirling around a glass of Shiraz. I, however, only visited Iran as a tourist, and in the early 'naughties', at that.

When Sassan moved to Tehran, Iran was in the throes of recovering from an eight-year-long war imposed by Saddam Hussein, and supported by the major Western powers alongside a number of Arab states. 'It was a tough place to be,' he remembered, 'really, really hard-core'. Ah, if only economic woes were what the young Sassan had to deal with. Being French-born and raised meant that he was looked at differently, as a 'European kid' and a foreigner, instead of as wholly Iranian; the situation is more or less the same today. As is the case with other Iranians who have grown up in the diaspora (yours truly included), Sassan's detractors claim that he has little credibility to speak about things such as the 'real' Iran, or even express an opinion. And what does he think of them? 'I don't consider them to be educated or to know what I'm trying to do on an international level. They're just jealous.'

Joobin Bekhrad

That Sassan is an angry young man is nothing new. It was anger (positive, albeit) that fuelled his desire to focus his creative energies in their entirety on Iran. 'The difficulties, funnily enough, turned me onto Iranian culture', he recalled with a smile. Though only a teenager with no memories of pre-Revolution Iran, Sassan could feel something in his bones and in the air. He felt a sense of nostalgia for eras he'd never experienced, perhaps much in the same way that the music of Googoosh evokes, for many young Iranians today, the halcyon days of their parents. Bored with school, and given the cold shoulder by many of his classmates, the soon-to-be artist began wandering about the streets of Tehran, digging beneath the sullied skin of the city for its beating heart. Taxi drivers and butchers became confidantes who provided the boy with a glimpse of post-Revolution realities and put things into perspective. 'My heart started bleeding for Iran', he told me, gazing glassy-eyed at the dwindling crimson elixir in his tumbler. He empathised with his new friends – most of who belonged to social strata far removed from his – and began, in his heart and mind alike, transmuting his frustration into a constructive force. His bedroom mirror reflected not the visage of a boy whose mouth still smelled of milk, but rather, a saviour-like figure. 'I could see myself leading people and inspiring them. Those experiences were the best thing that ever happened to me.'

* * *

'Maria! Come and look at his shoes! And those socks!'

My conversation with Sassan was pleasantly interrupted by the arrival of his wife, Maria, and their pug, Booboo. While Maria, his brother Ali, and his mother have all served as unflinching pillars of the House of Sassan, its namesake reminded me that as an artist, he has even had to prove himself amongst them. During the creation of the *Real Me* series, in which black-and-white photographs of the artist, as well as iconic Iranian landmarks and scenes (e.g. Persepolis and the *Si-o-Seh Pol* bridge in Esfahan) have been rent by vibrant, jagged streaks adorned with traditional Iranian motifs, Sassan's ideas were questioned not little by those around him. It was he, however, who relished the last laugh, the series having enjoyed a number of warmly received solo exhibitions and magazine features. 'Hah! *Now* you see', he said, grinning at Maria and tipping his glass to me with a nod.

While the battle has been won at home, Sassan – as in his childhood days – still struggles to get his messages across. Some look at the angry young man as delusional and out of touch with reality. While Booboo clawed at my legs in desperation, Sassan stroked back his flaxen mane and recalled an incident. 'Someone recently told me, "Sassan, we love your work, but the reality you show isn't the reality of the majority of Iranians today".' I was expecting him to flat-out disagree, and was taken aback at his answer. 'Of course it isn't – but it *can* be. I'm just giving you a glimpse of what Iran was and can be again.' Indeed, it was his disillusionment with the present state of Iran that, in many ways, birthed his artistic career. As such, one shouldn't be quick to deem Sassan a mere idealist, or one in denial. In listening to Sassan's comments about post-Revolution Iran, gazing at the massive stone lions at the entrance to his villa, and being confronted at every twist and turn inside by Achaemenid soldiers, it became clear what Sassan's ideals were as an Iranian. Though he hails from the Bakhtiar aristocracy, he doesn't long – as many Iranians in his position are wont to do – for the 'glory days' of the Pahlavis. Rather, he yearns for a return to ancient and indigenous Iranian roots, which he sees as having been tainted by outside influences; in other words, a return to an Iran before the fall of the House of Sassan. That being said, though, he maintains that his fight has nothing to do with race or religion, and instead everything to do with culture, nationalism, and the elevation of the hallowed name of Iran on the global stage. 'I want to show Iran to the most successful communities in the world,' he said, as we later drove past a villa belonging to Prince Albert of Monaco, 'because that's what we are – if not more'.

* * *

It was a mellow summer's evening in Saint-Jean-Cap-Ferrat. At the Four Seasons Hotel, a regular haunt of Sassan's, cool glasses of rosé wine were ordered in the spirit of the season. What I would have done, though, for a proper pint! As the soft strains of a violin came from beyond our table, draped in purest white, Sassan's words took on grander proportions. A few paintings and collages here and there are all fine and dandy, but they aren't going to get the neighbours to prick up their ears, and he knows it. It was then that the artist told me of his plans to establish a foundation dedicated to the promotion of contemporary Iranian art on an international level. Names of A-list individuals and venues were tossed around as if mere playthings. *Now you're talking*, I thought, as he veered between anger and excitement with the unbridled energy of a child. He'd show them, he said, that he was far more than just a French kid with his head in the clouds; he'd blow them out of the water, in fact, each and every one of them. It was as if he'd rehearsed every word he was telling me, so unflinching was he in his resolution, and so quick to quip at the slightest expression of doubt. He could see red carpets, towering chandeliers, the crème-de-la-crème of curators and who's-who's of the global contemporary art scene quaffing flutes of champagne from bottles blanketed in orange, all with the same blessed name on their lips: Iran. He could envision himself doing whatever he pleased, flashing and gnashing his teeth to spite the naysayers. 'I'm not doing this to make a name for myself … I'm doing this to support Iranian artists', he insisted, lest his intentions be misunderstood. *Well, I'll drink to that*, I thought. 'To the *Fondation*', I replied, echoing Sassan's words and clinking my pinkish-hued glass against his.

People can be so fickle. I'll give myself credit for having learned at least one thing from the time I've spent in the contemporary art scene. Out of sight, out of mind, here today, gone tomorrow. When I hugged Sassan before hopping in the taxi that would take me back to dark, dank England, I didn't think I'd ever talk to him again, let alone see him. It's become something of an instinct, a mechanism; one learns not to expect much of people, and to regard the world with the contempt of a dervish. When Sassan calls me these days, cruising somewhere along the coast of Monaco, it's usually to tell me of some new development concerning the *Fondation*: new works, bigger names, wilder parties. More often than not, he's burnt himself out working towards some event or other, or from heading the affairs of the Bakhtiar family. Perhaps he's more of a Bakthiar than he gives himself credit for; like those storied nomads, Sassan can never seem to sit still. He's restless to a fault, and owes much to this unrelenting condition of his. 'Sometimes I just want to turn this off,' he told me that evening, tapping his head, 'but I can't'.

* * *

Above me hangs, in a juicy-looking vermillion frame, a piece by Sassan entitled *Once Upon a Time, There Was Saddam.* My thoughts are dashing between the blood-strewn sands of Khorramshahr and the city of Bowie's heroes. I'm due to see Sassan in a few days. We won't be seeing each other in Saint-Jean-Cap-Ferrat this time, but rather, Berlin. Neither of us has been there, and Sassan is particularly excited about the prospect of going 'exploring'. Again, summertime; again, that season of wild abandon, sweaty palms, and wanderlust. And there we will be, a fair-haired French kid and a skinny boy from Toronto with funny socks, recalling dreams of yesteryear and lofty ambitions over blood-red wine, our hearts all the while in the land of the Lion and Sun.

10/8/2016

Joobin Bekhrad

An Absolute Beginner

It must have been around eight. Atusa had gone to get something from the corner store. She'd given the door a good slam and run as fast as her shiny heels could take her, shielding herself from the flurry of little hot shards grazing against her painted face. My hands were sweating; don't ask me why. I can't remember much about that evening, aside from the sky being purple. As I waited alone in her car, the glowing red digits fell back to zero and *Young Americans* bounced onto the stereo. I sank back into my seat, looking for a glimpse of Atusa but only spotting a sweeper, whose jaundiced eyes made me twitch my head towards the wasteland in the distance. What had kept her so long? Iranian girls drive me nuts. We were supposed to see the newlyweds – Atusa's sister, Anahita, and Kamran. I tried to forget the jokes my father had used to make about Kami, but to no avail. *Don't laugh, don't laugh,* I kept thinking to myself while straightening out my eyebrows in the rear-view mirror. 'What's so funny?' Atusa said as she opened the car door and tossed two plastic bags in the backseat. 'And what's this rubbish you're playing again? David … *chi chi?* What's his name?'

I laughed. I didn't, of course, tell anyone why; 'Nothing' was the best answer I could muster at the time. I could hear my mother in the back of my mind saying, *Vaa. Who laughs for no reason? People will think you're crazy*. Kami was smoking in a way that made him appear sleazier than usual, and, in the corner of my eye, I could see Anahita looking at me askance. Some moron with a perm was singing on a Persian satellite channel, and I was the only one who seemed to find it ridiculous. After an agonising half-hour of pistachios, tobacco, and drum machines, it was decided that we'd go our separate ways; Atusa and Anahita would get together with 'the girls', while Kami and I would take a spin. We would, he said, catch up with some friends of his who'd worked for him in the past (doing only God knows what). 'Nice girls,' he casually mentioned, exhaling with a squint a cone of smoke on the way to the underwhelming bar, 'Moroccans'. In my teenage mind, I did the math, and thought that perhaps my father had been right, after all. Maybe Kami really was a pimp.

It was kind of like that Smiths song, if one looked back on it like a dejected romantic; you know, the one about driving in a car and not having a home, *dadadadadada*. I wanted to forget all about 'her', and Kami knew it; Atusa had probably spilled the beans. I couldn't bear to think how two years ago, I'd stayed up all night in this city by the sea, endlessly thinking about her. Not much had changed by that point, really, except that I didn't have a godawful haircut or girly trainers anymore, and had kicked Johnny Rockets hamburgers for good. Though a pimp, his heart was in the right place; he wanted to show a pining adolescent a good time, and I didn't mind. I would have done anything to stay out that night, away from my father's empty bedroom and that old Spanish guitar, away from all those glittering dots and stars in the night sky that only made me feel so small up there on the twenty-fifth floor.

What were those leggy girls doing 'selling cars' for Kami? I didn't care, really. As long as 'she' wasn't on my mind, I was fine. *They're far prettier than her,* I thought. *Who needs her, anyway?* But whom was I fooling? I didn't want those Moroccan girls, no matter how red they made me blush. Besides, I had heard things about Moroccan women. 'Be careful,' someone had warned me, 'they make you fall in love with them, and you can never get away'. Why? 'Because, you see, they're into voodoo and black magic and all that. Don't say I didn't tell you!' No sir; I didn't feel like being turned into a voodoo doll anytime soon. I just wanted to be with her, wherever she was.

I couldn't tell whether they were coming on to me or just being nice; I've never been good at that sort of thing. What I did know was that the beer tasted better than ever, and that after a certain point I could no longer feel my legs. That must have been the first time I'd gotten pissed. Surprisingly, I didn't vow to never touch a drop again the following morning, despite feeling worse than that fellow with the perm had looked. Gone were the

Moroccan girls when I awoke; and, aside from the burning sensation in my head, I didn't feel as if any pins were being thrust into my limbs. It must have been three-ish. 'Tell me about it!' Kami afterwards remarked, as we sat together – I in my grungy blue jeans and he in his soiled wifebeater – watching Uma Thurman hack some Japanese guys to bits. 'There's this Chinese woman who brings me the best films.' I missed that old Spanish guitar more than ever then. He looked surprised when I asked to excuse myself. 'You're going to miss the best bit!' *Oh, what a pity.*

* * *

A waving flag. Cargo steamers. The blinding sun. Beige mounds upon roofs looking like baked sand dunes. The lure of the other side.

What am I doing here? I thought to myself, playing around with my wallet while the television spewed out the same old crap. I noticed something pink sticking to the back of a card: an underground ticket from London, valid for a day. It seemed like a vestige from a dream, like the one I'd had the other night. I'd dreamt I saw David in drag, with a hat that went flippity-floppity-flap. He'd patched up one eye, and had on these flowing blue robes. Our eyes met, not in the ballrooms of Mars or at some cosmic drive-in, but on the stairs at the Dubai International Airport. I put on a record, wondering when on earth nine o'clock would come. Atusa was still asleep, and the cleaning lady was humming something to herself in the kitchen. There wasn't even a book lying around to read, and certainly nowhere to go, save the hotel lobby with its ersatz everything and that ever-empty Damas store; and, ever since those prostitutes in their *abayas* had mistakenly knocked on our door one evening, the billowy spectres downstairs never quite looked the same.

Atusa and her friend Golnaz came around some hours later. On one end of my bed, I had the old guitar in hand, strumming in the cosy key of E, while on the other the two girls were chatting away about some boy or other. There was an 'Iranian night' going down that evening, which was fine – except for the fact that I was underage. I figured if I could escape voodoo, I could do anything, and so decided to wing it. In an attempt to smuggle me inside the sordid joint, Atusa smothered me against Golnaz, affording me the sensation of her sequins digging into my face. As soon as I got there, I wanted to leave. Five minutes in, I suddenly realised I'd been wearing the same pair of blue jeans for months on end. Everybody was dressed to the nines, and the sight of all those gorgeous things made me feel even more like a wandering schoolboy. Upstairs by the pool, some Armenian bloke named Samuel kept yelling at everyone to 'live it up', and an inebriated employee of my father's somehow got the idea that she could confide in me. For a good fifteen minutes or so, I was her stubbly saviour of the night, although I found myself at a loss for words when she started bawling. I couldn't blame her; I'd have been crying, too, had I found myself asking for advice from a wistful seventeen-year-old who'd just nicked a shirt from his dad's closet.

It was my last evening in Dubai, and I was feeling as hopeless as ever. I'm not sure whether that was because of my apprehensions about the future, or the nausea induced by the packet of Hardee's french fries I'd downed hours earlier. Perhaps both. Before us were those same stars and dots, glowing in our night sky, just as they were on that of the other side. In a few hours, I would be on a plane bound for the land of the Lion and Sun, for a place I have never been able to call 'home', yet which has always been the closest I've ever gotten to it. I wondered about the adventures Iran had in store for me that time, about all the places I'd go and the pretty girls I'd see. I knew I'd be down all the while, but didn't exactly fancy the thought of the life that awaited me back in Toronto. I wasn't sure how things would work out, or if they even would. I was happy that high school had finished (that's putting it lightly, really), but had never thought of what I'd do next. My feet flared up at the thought of where we'd both be, she and I, in two months' time. I thought I'd never see her again, and a little voice inside, fighting to be heard beneath all those french fries, told me I was probably right. *Iranian girls drive me nuts.*

Joobin Bekhrad

* * *

'Look at them … they look like models!' my father's business partner said, pointing at two sets of bronzed legs in miniskirts; such were his parting words at the airport the following afternoon. I was leaving Dubai again, and didn't know when I'd be back next. It mattered little, though; the other side was calling, pulling, dragging. In vain, I looked for a book to buy and kill some time with, but soon realised that it would be best to stick to my original plan of drowning myself in Costa coffee and drawing things on napkins. Sitting by myself, minding my own business, I remembered David and the stairs. I knew exactly where I'd seen him in my dream, and sought him on my way to the gate, burgundy passport in hand. He was nowhere in sight, and yet his image appeared all the same before me. Clad in drag and leaning on a gilded chestnut cane, his winsome smile on the brink of revealing a string of smoke-stained pearls, he gave me a wink from his one naked eye.

Hovering above the Zagros Mountains in the sky, I dozed off in the comforting thought that things would eventually sort themselves out. That's what David had tried to tell me, in his own way. *And if David believes so,* I thought, *does anything else matter?*

10/15/2016

Iran, 1970

Or, Persian Pictures: Gabriele Basilico on the Road in Iran

Torn white shirts, imbrued with caked blood and sweat. Raised fists pumping with vehemence, and the howls of underdogs piercing through concrete halls and cracked, blinding avenues. The memory of the sun during that long hot autumn still weighed heavily on their minds, and their scorched brows and roughened hands wouldn't let them, those street-fighting men and women, forget it. The butterflies had been let loose in London in memory of a wingless angel, and the last jagged nail had been driven home in the spartan coffin of a burnt-out dream. But they were young and hot-blooded yet; their eyes, though jaded and no longer sparkling with callow innocence, longed to see beyond those sleepy towns with their towering smokestacks, where death lay skulking in the shadows, breathing down necks and following in the footsteps of the dead-but-living. Ah, to be as free as a girl on a motorcycle, to ride out into the distance and watch the world shrink into nothingness behind you; and to keep riding, with no particular destination, chasing naught but the sun. The earth fetters only the feet of those who stand still, they thought; better to laugh at those sunken holes, to evade those cold fingers, and *move*. Happy those who die on the road, and not in their beds.

Joobin Bekhrad

* * *

A dusty drawer opened with a creak; a drawer that for nearly half a century had lain shut and unnoticed, its contents seemingly frozen in time, although occasionally warmed by that same sun of ages past. Illumined by its soft rays, images appeared in myriad shades of black and white. Little girls emerged, clutching swarthy *chadors* in their tiny fingers. There were patterns of confounding beauty, in the palaces of kings, in hallowed spaces, in the shepherd's flock, on the face of the earth itself. Grinning waifs, listless opium addicts, weary pedlars, and pilgrims lost in prayer inhabited a paradise of shadows and light, of visual poetry and perfect symmetry that at times seemed familiar, and at others, as distant as the dream that had brought those images into being.

With long unkempt locks, a sunburned face nestled in a beard, and a pair of greasy blue bellbottoms and sandals, Gabriele Basilico was a twenty-four-year-old architecture student when he and his friends decided to visit Iran. The year was 1970, and the plan was to venture far away from Milan, their studies, and the familiar, in search of a world less ordinary. Though studying architecture, Gabriele was slowly developing a penchant for photography. He knew, somehow, that the two cameras he always carried with him – one around his neck, and the other in his hand – would, like Giovanna, be with him until the very end. *Ex*

Oriente lux, he thought whilst spinning around a globe, wondering where to go. He knew that all things had their beginning and end in the East, in the land of the rising sun. It was soon decided, therefore, that they would follow the flower-strewn spice route to faraway Kabul and Samarkand, to the realms of Zarathustra and Mani, of fire, light, and Persian blue.

* * *

And so it happened that one sunny morning on the coast of the Venetian Riviera, Gabriele and Giovanna set off in his father's rickety Fiat 124 with little more than wanderlust and just enough to see them through to the other side of the world: jerry cans filled with water and gasoline, a sleeping tent for two, inflatable mattresses, and a stove, which, in addition to other odds and sods, they had picked up from the Fiera di Sinigaglia market. Aside from their hearts and the open road to guide them, they also took along with them a ruffled Michelin guide and cut-outs of photographs from a copy of *National Geographic*, which would lead them to the troglodyte cave dwellings of Cappadocia in central Turkey. He would first cut his teeth there, he thought, and make a name for himself as a budding photographer after selling his images to a local Italian newspaper. 'Mmm … Cappadocia', he said to himself. 'They'll go wild.'

Joobin Bekhrad

Bumping along in the Fiat across Europe, it was all
hunky-dory, too close to home: clouds of smoke
above towering chimneys, crumbling factories and
warehouses, the plight of the proletariat; but, as
they rolled into Istanbul with Leo, Claudia, Paola,
and Franco, whom they'd caught up with in
Dubrovnik, Gabriele felt as if the visions and
spectres he'd often seen during those sleepless
nights, during which he'd writhe between his sheets
and stare, hopelessly, outside his window, were
taking shape. *If only we'd come by sea!* Young
Gabriele would have, like his compatriot de Amicis
before him, seen minarets obscured by fog, the
hazy outline of cupolas on the horizon, gulls
circling above choppy, limpid waves, and rolling
hills speckled with white, red, and ochre. He would
have joined all the others to rush out, agog, onto
the deck to fathom the unfathomable:
Constantinople, of Byzantium that was once theirs,
and now lost to even the Grand Signor himself.

But the dream, they all knew, lay further eastwards.
It was no time for dawdling and indulging in
fantasies; from afar resounded the call of Persia, of
Khorasan and Kharazm. He would venture
beyond de Amicis and Bon, who had perhaps
become too accustomed to the splendours of
Ottoman court culture and the manifold quarters
of Stamboul, which to them must have seemed like
the sordid beating heart of the world, teeming with
every people under the sun: Persians, Greeks,
Armenians, Venetians, Jews, and – in the eyes of

the Italian travellers – the nefarious Turk, whose insolent armies had dared to penetrate so far as into the Holy Roman Empire, up to the gates of Vienna herself! No, Gabriele wasn't following in the footsteps of those curious Italians, but rather in those of another young traveller from the westerly shores of Europe. Forty years before him, a twenty-something Robert Byron had set out from Albion to visit a Persia under the iron grip of Marjoribanks, and Afghanistan, ravenous to devour, with wide and wanting eyes, the architecture of the Persianate world. Like Gabriele would after him, the twenty-eight-year-old Byron had documented part of his journey in the form of black-and-white photographs; unlike the Latin, however, Byron had managed to journey further eastwards to Afghanistan, where he encountered a people whose authenticity, vis-à-vis that of their Persian cousins and their faux-Western ways, captivated him. Nay – thirsty for Samarkand and Kabul, the sun-worshippers never made it past the land of lovers, world-conquerors, and wild dervishes. Blame it on a Citroën.

* * *

Sitting at the wheel of his father's fading Fiat, his hands moist from perspiration and his fair cheeks rough and ruddy, Gabriele felt ill. Perhaps he'd caught something in one of the roadside hovels they'd been stopping at along the way; or, he thought as he tugged at his beard in anxiety, he might have been burning out. He couldn't remember the last time he'd had a proper meal, and the thought was enough to make him long for the Milan he had only been too fain to get away from. A diet of peaches, water, and kebabs had done a number on him and Giovanna, and, passing by the restaurants lining never-ending Pahlavi Avenue, he blushed at his jealousy. But by then, he had gotten used to a stoic life on the move and the way of the rolling stone; being skint and hungry for adventure meant that you clawed at whatever came your way, and thanked the man, too. No, it wasn't those godawful peaches or the stifling heat under a sun that 'just wouldn't die', as he'd heard some say; it was something more unnerving, more nauseating – something he knew all too well, and which had seemingly followed the gang all the while: the odious stench of globalisation. They sickened him, those 'modern' women in their fuck-me pumps who spoke French and wanted to eat Alain Delon alive, those boys in whose eyes one could see American dreams and fantasies of laying blonde, blue-eyed bimbos, those slavish parvenus who were ready to bow to anyone with so much as a smattering of a British or American accent. He hadn't come all the way from Milan to drink Pepsi Cola and see Lando Buzzanca on the silver screen; where was the Iran of his dreams, of the tales of Scheherazade, of Gathic hymns? Were these 'Westoxified' children really the heirs of the Shahs who had used Roman emperors as footstools and made Pharaohs grovel on bended knee? That wasn't his scene; but he knew they were there, the Iranians of old, the 'dignified and simple boys with their beautiful necks, the beautiful, bright faces under innocent haircuts'[1], as Pasolini would later describe them.

* * *

'To hell with this lot', he muttered under his breath, tapping his sticky fingers along to a ditty on the radio. He wanted to see the grittier parts of Tehran in the south that one often saw in those tough-guy movies; and from Tehran, he resolved to travel not further east, but south towards the Persian Gulf, to the ruins of what was once the most splendid palace on earth, the crushing epicentre of the storied empire that had long ago, guided by the fire of Mazda and the Holy Immortals, held the world in its sway. Perhaps, away from 'frenetic' Tehran, the seekers thought, would they find those beautiful children of noble blood they so sought.

The dog-eared Michelin guide, warped and curled by heat and sweat, suggested they first visit the holy city of Qom on their southern expedition. The locals didn't know what to make of the gaunt *farangi* in his bellbottoms, snapping pictures of scowling, sun-baked faces around the shrine of the Innocent. 'Maybe he's a Georgian or Armenian', whispered some in the deep shadows of the sumptuous minarets; they were dead giveaways, the six curious travellers who found themselves in the wrong place at the wrong time. They weren't after the mythical treasures of the shrine, whose whereabouts one of their rascally countrymen, an infidel disguised in billowing Persian robes, had once hastily scrawled down in a frayed notebook, as some may have thought; nor did they, by way of some sinister ruse, intend to bring misery upon the faithful of Fatemeh. But it mattered little when they caught a glimpse of those foreboding glares and the man with the blackened brow reaching for a stone that would fit his gnarled palms. 'It would be best if you left', a policeman told them brusquely; well then, step on the gas and wipe that tear away. *In any case*, they thought, *there's not a bite to be had here, and our peaches are turning to mush. Toss that bastard guide out the window; we'll just keep driving, keep moving, onwards towards… Oh! Esfahan, the Image of the World itself, Shiraz, the city of poets…*

* * *

We have no peaches. Our pockets are empty, our faces desiccated and burnt, and our soles hard and heavy; but in beholding thee, Esfahan, we feel not our burden, but an ineffable hope and elation. In you, the Image of the World, we see not this ever-wandering sphere, suspended in the Cimmerian void above, but Paradise as your sleeping children once envisioned it on brumal steppes and in the windswept deserts of Persia. A symmetry so sublime, so terrifyingly ethereal, and – Dio mio – grand beyond belief; even had I not eyes would I feel your beauty and presence, so palpable are they. I have come home, home to my East, in which all things have their beginning and end. I can see it all: all worlds merge in you, Esfahan, genius of the Persian psyche and soul. On the surface of thy holy houses, I see shimmering fairy-tale domes and humbling ivans dripping with stalactites in a hundred colours, and pulpits from the ages of hordes; but the deeper I dig, the more I search, the more your essence becomes apparent, O Iran, land of the noble. I hear echoes of the House of Sassan through chambers of Achaemenid stone, and the hooves of chargers, foaming at the mouth, from beyond the Oxus; I feel the warmth of Zarathustra's flame, that spark of Mazda burning yet, and see everywhere the bluest blue, of the earth of Khorasan and that elixir the Persians have ever held dear. Yea, Esfahan, thou truly art the image of this world and the next.

* * *

Another fever had come on; this time, though, Gabriele knew it was different. Sweating through a threadbare button-down shirt that had seemingly been to hell and back, his head, buffeted by hot gusts of wind, throbbed with a million different thoughts. Had they been real, Esfahan and Shiraz? They seemed so far away, though their kaleidoscopic images lingered yet. He hadn't understood any of the strange, beautiful verses of the tongue of the unseen, incanted as if they were the arcana of some coterie or other; but he could feel their imprint on his heart all the same. He had changed. His being had been kissed by the hot

Persian sun, he had been unwittingly initiated into a fraternity of poets and mystics. The warp and weft of his sense of time and space had, without the smoke of flowers, shifted, and things he had once thought trivial began to take on, in his knowing eyes, a new and profound significance. The thought gave him a jolt; as they passed a string of roadside inns and the crumbling ruins of an old caravanserai amidst burnt plains and purple mountains, he began to realise what was happening to him: the inevitable that happens to all who tarry in the land of the Lion and Sun. He was becoming Persian. Looking outside the window of the bumbling Fiat, a grin stretched out across his hardened face. '*Che?*' his friends asked him. '*Niente*', he replied, still smiling, fancying that he could see the ghost of Della Valle, bedecked in sumptuous Persian garb, winking at him in the distance.

Onwards, ever onwards. Ruin after ruin, nomads with their flocks and swarthy goat-hair tents, the sun beating down harder than ever before. He could feel it in his bones, smell it in the hot, dusty air: they were nearing Persepolis. The very idea of being in the presence of that fallen city, whose name he couldn't help but whisper over and over again to himself, made him realise his own insignificance, and brought on a feeling of bitter remorse. He cursed the wild Macedonian, who, in a drunken rage destroyed that which he had so envied and desired; but, more than the Iranophile and his Greeks-turned-Persian, he railed in his heart against savage time, who had forgotten the dream of Darius and left his gilded utopia in a heap of dust and rubble. The abode of the proud *Homa* bird and those towering winged bulls had been ransacked by shameless wolves and jackals. Who could have ever fathomed such an idea, such a dream, and pulled it off with such pomp? Had you asked the locals centuries ago, they would have sworn it was the work of the mythical Jamshid, whose bejewelled goblet had held the secrets of the universe – no, it couldn't have been the work of a mere mortal, however much he had been smiled upon by Mazda on high. As those broken pillars, burning naked on the horizon – not unlike the decaying smokestacks of Milan – came into view, he thought of the old potter he'd seen whilst meandering in the shadows of an Esfahani alleyway, and the words of a wise tentmaker: *He made them sturdy – handles, lids, and all – from the hands of tramps, and the heads of kings*[2].

* * *

'There will be an imperial dinner, plates of pasta unseen even in Rome, and, in the evening, the magical, sights, sounds, and lights of an extraordinary archaeological site'[3], an Italian official told the travellers in Persepolis. A year later, the most extravagant celebration the modern world had ever seen, or could remember, would cast a dark shadow over the Light of the Aryans and herald the beginning of the end. Amidst a coruscating crowd of emperors, figureheads, and petty dictators, Cyrus, the Father, would be told to sleep at ease; for the Shah of Iran, ever-powerful and adored by the leaders of worlds civilised and barbarian – who would pass in supplication through the Gate of All Nations, like their forefathers twenty-five hundred years ago – rested firmly atop the Peacock Throne. Were they omens, those spiralling clouds of dust? The faulty fireworks? Those little Spanish birds that fell from atop transplanted trees, unable to withstand the scorched earth of the Persian heartland?

The greatest show on earth had, perhaps, *roused* Cyrus from his slumber; for the spirit of Cyrus, like Gabriele, would have found little to revel in and celebrate. Cyrus, whose praises Gabriele had read in Machiavelli and his ancient Greek texts, would have known that those the Shah was so impassionedly endeavouring to impress would soon desert him – or worse – lay siege to his beloved Iran at the first opportunity. And, like Gabriele, Cyrus' heart would have sunk at the sight of such stinging distinctions of class, and the abject poverty of his children, downtrodden and miserable, for whom he had fought to build an empire and elevate to the highest spheres. One can only imagine how Cyrus, with his finger pressed against his lip, would have felt at the sight of his descendants, tearing off their clothes in the name of progress, salivating in awe at the sight of those from the West – the glorious, infallible West – and desperately striving to ape their every move. *Nay,* Cyrus' blessed spirit must have been crying from the House of Song, *for this I did not give my head.*

Gabriele knew, and could feel that the Iran of Cyrus and his bedroom visions was slowly being effaced by the unstoppable plague of 'Westoxification'. Just as he was witnessing how the old abandoned edifices of Italy were giving way to modern ones more befitting of a world looking towards the moon and the approaching millennium, so too did he see the indigenous and ancient ways of the Iranians slowly crumbling before a largely imposed idea of modernity and imported ideals. To be traditional, or Iranian, was passé; though Iranian identity was being redefined and re-examined, and the bourgeois were wallowing in fantasies of their nation's heyday, Iranian eyes and hearts alike were leaning increasingly westwards, to Europe and the New World. 'She's beautiful … she looks just like those foreigners with blue eyes and blonde hair … *just like a foreigner.*'[4] The modern-day Darius dreamed not of Persian glories, but taking Farah Fawcett lookalikes to San Francisco.

* * *

Talk about a rude awakening, Gabriele thought to himself upon arriving in Milan, one hand in Giovanna's and the other clutching a Hasselblad.

Joobin Bekhrad

The dream was over; they had seen their East and made their pilgrimage to the source of the sun, following no dictate save that of ever moving forward and evading the spectres clinging to their heels. At customs, their belongings were gutted and a pound of not the opium of their hollow-cheeked friends, but henna, seized from them. They would never see Iran again, nor would they ever set their eyes on Kabul and Samarkand. Even if he were to visit Iran again, he was certain it wouldn't be the same; as always, the old would dwindle before the new, and all around would ring slogans of progress, civilisation, and reform. It would only be a matter of time before his Iran would be dashed to pieces by He who maketh and breaketh, the Potter. At least, he thought, scratching his cheeks through the curls of his beard, he had his little pictures to tell the tale of what once was, and what would never again be.

3/22/2016

Bibliography

1. Nollet, D. *Iran, in the Shadow of an Immobile Reality* [online]. Accessed 19 May 2016. Available from: http://www.cape. ag/?p=649.
2. Bekhrad, J. *The Quatrains of Omar Khayyam.* Bloomington: Balboa Press, 2017.
3. Doninelli, L., Gabriele Basilico, and Giovanna Calvenzi. *Iran 1970.* Milan: Humboldt Books, 2015.

4. Faryad Zir-e Ab [film]. Directed by Sirus
   Alvand. Iran: Panasit, 1977.

Joobin Bekhrad

Seeing Red
The art of Reza Derakshani

He stood there, motionless before the rusty microphone, not knowing what to do with his tanned, wiry hands. A haze of smoke and flowers lingered about in the air, and, in the corner of his eye, he could make out the longhair delicately rolling a joint and smacking his lips. He didn't make too much of it at first, just as he hadn't recognised the fellow in the corner after the gig at the boozer in town. It came on like a slow burn, like some supernal, numbing high, inching its way up his knees towards his damp navel and rumbling viscera. A spate of blurred images rushed past his eyes: shining leather trousers, a woman from the city of angels, drawn-out afternoons spun away by hot, scratched vinyl, the glow of blood-red pomegranates. It was then that it hit him: how had he come all that way, from the sleepy village of Sangsar, to be where he was at that particular moment in time? His hands moist, he awkwardly grappled with the forlorn microphone before clearing his throat with a curt cough. Once, many moons ago, an American poet had howled into the same hunk of metal before him, telling tales of loneliness, bacchanalia, and rapture; but, as soon as he opened his mouth, the phantom of old Jim fizzled away into those folds of smoke, out of which appeared that of the bard of Shiraz, kindler of hearts. He could feel his knees again; with eyes closed, looking inwards towards a warm, lambent space, he remembered what the stars looked like atop the Alborz Mountains.

He remembered the stars, and days of insouciance and idleness on the outskirts of Damavand near bustling Tehran. It was in his blood, and written on his forehead: as an Iranian, he would always be a nomadic soul on the move. Come the summertime, his family would head towards the pastures of idyllic Damavand, while in the wintertime, they would make for Sangsar in the east. There, in Damavand, were only fields of flowers, black tents, snowy mountaintops, and plains of grass on which the sheep would feed; for the sheep, as they all knew, *must live*. In the shadow of his father, who appeared to his child's eye a 'Persian cowboy', he found confidantes in stray dogs, and atop wild horses could espy in the silence of dawn the peak of mighty Damavand itself. Only later, as with the microphone, would he realise the significance of it all – the horses, the ancient tongue of the nomads, the state of constant movement; he was continuing in the tradition of his ancient forebears, who had set out from their Aryan homeland towards the realm that would come to be known as 'Iran'.

Even then, riding astride rufous mares in what seemed to him to be the middle of nowhere, he knew he wanted to be an artist. Perhaps it had to do with his picturesque surroundings; or, it may have been a desire born out of necessity. His father, soon enough, found himself penniless, and, as the sheep needed to survive, so did the boys. His older brother, an artist and a teacher, set an example for him. It was also then discovered that the lad had a voice, which, during those hot, dusty evenings in the countryside, reduced the womenfolk to tears. By the age of twelve, the young boy was not only painting reproductions of European masterpieces commissioned by clients, but also works of his own that surprised even him. By this time, his family had moved again, albeit to less bucolic environs. Initially, they settled in perfumed Neyshapur, but later moved to Sabzevar, and finally, Semnan. There, beneath the stifling sun, he felt like Van Gogh himself, as he whiled away lazy afternoons painting the ancient landscape.

The next move he would make would not be elsewhere in the Iranian heartland, but on, as he and those around him used to call it, 'the other side of the water'. After finishing his BA degree at Tehran University, he decided to pursue higher education in Los Angeles; but, unluckily, he found himself in the wrong place at the wrong time. Back home, a million miles away, there had been a revolution. The King of Kings had flown away in a white jet plane, and in his stead had come the man on the moon in flowing chestnut robes. Things were getting heavy, and fast. Before he knew it, there would be a hostage crisis involving his country and the land of milk and honey, and soon afterwards, a war, which, although instigated by Saddam Hussein, would degenerate into one between the *world* and Iran. The ones they would call 'fearless Iranians from Hell' would walk on mines and throw themselves onto tanks, while their star-spangled brethren would enjoy life as personae non grata. Though his homeland would later be in vogue again (at least from an artistic perspective), things at the time weren't exactly *gol-o-bolboli*. Iranians simply weren't appreciated, he found, even in cultural centres like New York City. Though in the thick of his studies, he ditched university and did perhaps the only other thing he knew: move. And so, during the first year of the Iran-Iraq War, with Khorramshahr ravaged and awash in its own blood, he left sunny Los Angeles for Tehran.

The stint in the Iranian capital was short-lived. Feeling again the urge to ramble, he, along with his wife and son, left for Los Angeles. This time, the move was not as linear; en route to the States, the family stopped over in Italy, the only place where they could obtain a fifteen-day travel visa; but, instead of staying for two weeks, they ultimately ended up living in Italy for a year with almost nothing and not even a place to rent. In the spirit of Khayyam, the cupbearer was nevertheless called, and the wine poured forth. *Why lament tomorrow's misfortunes today?* Eventually, the trio made it to Los Angeles, although only six months later, he would set out again for Italy. New York City would become the closest thing to 'home' for an uncharacteristically long sixteen years, even though he'd move yet again, and again, and again. Down and out in the Big Apple, he couldn't even afford to rent a studio, as a result of which he began to focus more on his music. All he needed to record was his *tar*, a small room, and a heart brimming with the blues. And boy, did he have the blues.

* * *

He had always liked the shape of that thing, the *tar*. Oblong and smooth, he enjoyed the feeling of its round bowl pressing against his stomach, no matter however much it was prone to slip down his thighs. At an early age, he had made a connection with the masters of classical Persian music, and soon began connecting the dots. In his teenage mind, the difference between Qamar-ol-Molook Vaziri and Janis Joplin was only superficial. They were the same emotions, the same feelings that were being expressed; it was simply the outward form of the music that struck his ear as different. *What of the husk? The kernel seize!* After *tar* lessons, during which he studied the *radif* repertoire, he would play Pink Floyd and Doors records in his bedroom. Standing there before the microphone, he remembered how he had once idolised Jim Morrison, whose decaying apparatus he was holding between his sweaty hands. His whines and wails were a far cry from those village verses that had gathered tears; but, just as he had always been a nomad at heart, so too had he been a rock and roller.

Beneath the hot white lights of the stage, he struck and swung around his diminutive *setar* with all the abandon and swagger of the rock and roll star he'd always wanted to be. That night in New York City, he was expressing the musical equivalent of a fulsome 'fuck you' to a crowd of New Age poets, charlatans, and pseudo-intellectuals. Quite naturally, then, was he caught unawares when he put a face to the sound of a gaunt moustachioed member of the crowd who introduced himself backstage. It was, he later found out, none other than John Densmore, the man who had provided the backbeat and drive to Morrison's unrestrained ecstasy. Fiddling around with a *daf* frame-drum he found lying around, chains and all, he and Densmore soon broke out into a jam and hit it off. Later, spurred by his desire to collaborate with the rock and roller and Densmore's interest in 'authentic' Persian music, the duo recorded albums and played a string of concerts together to much acclaim. It was during one of these heady days that he found himself feeling like jelly before the old microphone and its patina of sweat and rust. *You've come all the way from Sangsar,* he thought to himself that afternoon, *and you're singing into Jim Morrison's microphone. Ey Khoda!*

* * *

Life, he admitted, was good. Things had picked up in the art department, and he was rocking with the greats. He had a proper studio of his own, and, to all outward appearances, wanted for nothing. In the same little depth of his being, though, in which he could see clearly the stars shining atop Mount Damavand, he also saw arched eyebrows, towering cypresses, and everywhere, *red:* the red of the lover's rose, of the pomegranate, of houses of baked clay, of the 'Bloody City', Khorramshahr.

He didn't have any expectations; in fact, he didn't know *what* to feel. It seemed like ages since he'd been in Tehran, and there, knee-deep in the quotidian pandemonium of its leafy, soot-stained streets, he felt as if only those mountains, ever looming in the distance, were familiar. *Hell,* he thought when he was offered a solo exhibition in the capital, *I don't even have a passport.* Things were arranged, though, and not only did he receive a gold-imprinted burgundy document allowing him to travel to all but Occupied Palestine, but was also met by an unlikely reception. Maybe it was something in the air, the smell of change, of better things to come; it was, after all, the Khatami era. Regardless, they loved him there. New York City had become 'home', but he wasn't one to forget his roots. He knew he'd come from those mountains, those stony monoliths whose traces streaked through his bones. By their foothills, he had seen the stars for the first time; and though he was always on the move, they followed his every footstep. The stars, he felt, didn't look the same anywhere else, though they weren't any different. To see them, he knew he'd always have to return to Tehran, to Damavand, to *Iran*.

His peregrinations almost got the better of him there, but he couldn't bring himself to move again. He was jealous, almost, of his compatriots in Tehran; they all had their own studios, and were enjoying the luxury of having their own solo exhibitions. They didn't know how much they'd had it made. But there were words left unsaid, words that *couldn't* be said, and lines that could only be crossed once. In his mind, deciding to stay there was the artistic equivalent of committing suicide. New York, cold and grey on the other side of the world, was calling; again, he would be torn from his beloved mountains. He didn't know where he belonged, or what had been etched upon his brow in the crucible of time. He only knew, as he looked down on his manic beloved metropolis from way up high, awash in incandescent daubs of orange and yellow, that he would miss those stars.

* * *

Isn't it funny? he thought, fidgeting with a cigarette he was trying to light against the wind one cold morning, *You don't realise how much you love a place until you leave it.* Walking on the dirty boulevard, he felt like Johnny. He saw those horses with their big black eyes, *coming in in all directions*, in all imaginable colours. The ashen skyscrapers before him gave way to the mountains – *his mountains* – and all around him, voices whirled in Sanskrit and Avestan, hailing daevas and damning them at once, singing the hymns of the Gathas. There, buffeted by the wind in bleak Manhattan, he felt as if he were riding with the nomads of Sangsar, with the ancient Indo-Iranians themselves in Aryanam Vaejah. They were atop the very steeds, which, chained to the chariot, enabled them to conquer and give their name to Iran. But why such urgency? What were they after, and wherefore were they tugging at their bowstrings? Ah! In awe, he dropped his half-burnt cigarette by the curb. The hunt!

He was running back to his apartment, but couldn't feel his legs; it wasn't them that were carrying him, but some supernatural force that swept him away with the fervour of a dream gone wrong. He could only see a thousand horses, the white peaks of the Alborz Mountains, and glowing apertures in the sky. He arrived home in a lather and instinctively made for his studio. Frenzied, he knocked aside the cans of paint on the racks onto the mottled floor. 'No, not that one', he whispered beneath his breath in frustration. He had only one colour in mind: *red.* But it wasn't just any shade of red that would do, that would capture that euphoria and hallowed madness. He had seen it in the wanderings of his mind. *The red of the lover's rose,* he thought, *of pomegranates, of houses of baked clay …* He had only one wish, then, during a moment not when sons forget their mothers, as is said, but when lovers lose sight of the stars: to drown himself in the deepest red, to paint a thousand horses, to drink the Magian draught and sink his teeth in the daughter of the vine …

* * *

The smoke hanging thick and heavy in the viscid air, he opened the book he'd brought along to a page at random. The man in the corner cast an inquisitive glance, but he was blind to all around him – even Jim's battered microphone. Resting his yellowed, slender fingers on the undulating, dotted curves before him, he closed his eyes and sang the song he had been born to sing:

Ravished hath my heart become, and I, dervish unaware,
Know not why yon ravenous wanderer setteth her snare.
Like a willow do I tremble, losing my faith to the breeze;
That arch-browed infidel hath my worrying heart seized.
Oh! I feel the need to ramble, to make for that rumbling sea;
What secrets lie within this drop? Impossible 'tis to perceive.
May I caress that wisp of sorrow, that coy, winsome lash,
From which floweth her elixir in life-bestowing draughts.
A hundred drops of blood drip from my beloved's sleeve;
Her hand, even steady, doth mine aching heart aggrieve.
Weeping and downcast, to the tavern I make my way;
Why, at the thought of such affairs, do I feel this shame?
Neither shall Khezr live forever, nor Alexander's realm remain;
To trouble thyself with this worthless world – why, dervish, deign?
Not every back, Hafez, bendeth towards the hand of the beggar;
Seek thou the riches worth more than Korah's treasure!

– From the *Divan* of Hafez (translated by the author) *3/14/2016*

Joobin Bekhrad

Children of the Revolution

I tried to remember, but I couldn't. It was one of
those moments, when, provoked by a melody,
smell, or dream he'd had the previous night, and
plunged into contemplation by some distraction –
the inching away of a moist cigar in the sun,
transient clouds of *ghalyan* smoke obscuring the
sight of the Persian Gulf in the distance, the
warmth afforded by a singeing tumbler of cognac
– my father would recall someone, something,
someplace. To be more precise, it was the eve of
the vernal equinox, the night of *Norooz*, when, after
all the fires have been lit, winter is bid farewell and
spring welcomed with the blast of the cannon and
the serpentine whine of the *zorna*. But there hadn't
been any bonfires, and not a sound was to be heard
on the lonely streets outside.

He was sitting before me, glassy-eyed, while around
us resonated the metallic jangle of Farhad's steel-
string guitar. What a man, that Farhad. My father
used to tell me stories of how he and his brother
were amongst the few that Farhad would allow to
sit at his table at the Koochini club where he sang
– perhaps owing to their friendship with the club's
main man, Jalal (a.k.a. 'Jimi'). There, with his
bushy hair and moustache, cleaved button-down
shirt revealing a tangle of chest hair and
shimmering pendants, and his eyes ever-closed, he
would sing of bloody Fridays, fallen sparrows, and

lonely hearts. It was only from afar, though, that his husky voice resounded, rolling 'r's and all.

With these, do I bring winter to an end; with these, do I weariness forfend. With what, Farhad? I have sung your song a thousand times, like a child, on sleepy London streets after the rain, but it feels as distant as a dream yet. Still, every now and then, do I have to ask my father about those lanterns, those banging spoons, those little wooden sticks. 'What days we had', said my father, fighting against the lump in his throat, 'what sweet *Norooz* memories. Everyone's gone.' I was there, watching my parents wipe away tears from their stinging eyes, listening to Farhad and his guitar, at once knowing and dumbfounded. I wished I could imagine the sights and sounds whirling around in their heads, or at least, a story to call my own. But I – a gangly Hyrcanian a million miles away from home – couldn't. God knows I tried to remember, but I just couldn't.

* * *

He sees him every night, in his dreams, behind veils of white satin. He knows he's gone, but they banter and bicker nonetheless, as if nothing's changed. Perhaps he isn't really gone, just as Farhad isn't, or Grandma and Grandpa. Yes, if you close your eyes and think hard enough, you can imagine Maman Aziz sweeping the house at five in the morning, Baba Nosrat reading the paper, cursing clerics under his breath, and *Amoo* Mehrdad wiping the sweat from his brow in Bandar Mahshahr. *We'll see them all again soon; just think as if there aren't any telephone lines.* 'You would have loved to hang out with your dad and uncle, wouldn't you?' my mother asked me. All I could do was nod with a faint smile; for all I have are my father's stories and a handful of photographs. One in particular has always been my favourite. My uncle Mehrdad, fourteen, has plastered Winston cigarette cartons on his otherwise run-of-the-mill suit, just before a costume party, at which there'll be Stones records, booze, and pretty girls aplenty. There's a playful look in his eyes, as if he can perfectly imagine, down to the last detail, the escapades to come. My father always tells me that I remind him of his brother, my body, attitude, and love of certain things bearing an uncanny resemblance to his. I'll have to take his word for it; my uncle passed away when I was only ten years old. I never got the chance to see him.

I often find myself lying on my bed and looking at that photograph, trying to imagine not only the adventures of my uncle and father in Tehran in the seventies, but also the stories of others like them, during those hot and heady days. For as long as I can remember, my parents have been telling me that they left Iran for my sake, and that I should always be thankful I never grew up there, but rather, in Canada, the 'greatest country in the world'. Whenever I'd get bored as a little boy, I'd quickly be reminded of the other kids in Iran who had 'nothing to do'. An image soon formed in my mind of little tin shacks in a rainy wasteland, where ragamuffins played with pebbles and stones. As a child, Iran meant little to me; it was merely the name of a godforsaken country my parents and I were originally from. I was a Parsi school dropout, and proud of it. Who had time for stories of villagers and talking birds when there was the usual drudgery of homework to be done, cartoons to be watched, and rock and roll songs to be played on an old tennis racquet? Only years later, when the flames of love had been kindled and those of ignorance snuffed out, would I realise what a fool I'd been, and yearn for what I'd never had. Alright – Canada was 'heaven on earth'; but I couldn't stop thinking, alone in my bedroom, what life would have been like had I grown up in my beloved Iran, shoulder to shoulder with my brethren, my kith and kin, the children of the Revolution.

Who were they, those children of the Revolution? As when I think of my uncle and grandparents, I rest my head on my pillow, close my eyes, and wander in the whorls of my imagination. They were children, dressed like Farhad and my uncle, who loved rock and roll and wanted to be like Behrouz Vossoughi. Angry young men and women with blood-stained palms and placards fighting in the streets. Little boys with nothing but faith and their bare hands, who lunged at tanks and willingly walked on mines in the name of Iran. Children who arose to the sound of sirens, and came of age feeling, somehow, that they'd been ripped off. Children who waved bloodied shirts as banners and painted their faces green – in anger, desperation, and above all, unflinching hope. They'd been burned, but at least had their stories to tell. I had none.

* * *

One afternoon, at precisely a quarter to three in the afternoon on the thirteenth of Mordad, Saeed fell in love with Leyli. My father and uncle, on the other hand, were roaming about on Pahlavi Avenue with Oshnos dangling from their supple lips, eyeing doe-eyed belles in miniskirts. Ebi and Shahram Shabpareh would be singing with the Black Cats at the Koochini club, but the brothers knew that the evening would most probably degenerate into a drunken revel, during which Ebi and Shahram would start singing nonsense for the hell of it, and a bucket of ice would come pouring down on the head of Raj, the brawny doorman. Abadan, the Anglicised Persian Gulf city where they'd grown up, had been fun, but Tehran was something else; it was, after all, *the capital of Iran*. And what a throbbing, sordid, and sleazy hotpot of a capital it was. You could drink (or smoke) whatever you wanted, screw whomever caught your fancy, and top things off with a soft-core French flick at the local cinema and a round of genuflexions at the mosque. Live and let live was the rule all and sundry swore by – as long as you didn't step beyond your rug, as the saying goes. The Shah – the Light of the Aryans, God's Shadow on Earth – was a frizzy-haired prophet who enjoyed skiing in the Alps and living it up in Monaco; placed on the Peacock Throne by the Americans and the Brits (who later helped him give the nationalist Prime Minister, Dr Mohammad Mossadegh, a fine thrashing), he was unquestionable, unerring, and beyond reproach in every way; indeed, he was the very *ensan-e kamel* so lauded by the likes of Rumi and the great medieval Persian mystics. The land of the noble was ruled by one man, and one man alone, who, through the only permissible political party – the *Rastakhiz* (Resurrection) – held it in the same iron grip with which his father before him had snatched away Iran from the debauched Qajars. Not only the Shah, but also anything having even the remotest connection to him and the Pahlavi government, was off-limits. With SAVAK's notoriety on the rise, and the Shah's vision of a secular, highly Westernised Iran echoing the glory days of Cyrus the Great and the Achaemenids becoming increasingly detached from reality, many felt wronged, betrayed, and outright humiliated – particularly those unlucky enough to have been born far from Tehran's swanky northern suburbs in the grittier south, or worse, outside Tehran altogether in the 'sticks'.

Joobin Bekhrad

The lavish, over-the-top celebrations for the twenty-five hundredth anniversary of the founding of the Persian Empire by Cyrus the Great in 1971, many have said, sounded the death knell for the Pahlavis. There, amongst the mighty ruins of what was once the capital of the world, the Shah saw himself as Cyrus' heir, and the sole individual keeping Iran together as a unified whole, on whom Iranians depended. Beyond the circles of the elite by the foothills of the Alborz Mountains, Iran – much like it was during the dark days of the Qajars – was for the most part a wretched nation mired in poverty, illiteracy, and social inequality, amongst other malaises, although the bourgeoisie and aristocracy seldom deigned to admit it. But, however dim the light of Mithras and Mazda then seemed, the children of the Revolution – the brood of Cyrus and Zarathustra, with fire in their hearts and dust on their sunburnt faces – felt as if they were on the brink of a new dawn and era, emboldened by words that smelled of blood and the sight of the full moon.

* * *

They dropped their guitars, tossed on a pair of threadbare blue bellbottoms, and took to the streets. While the Shah reclined in breezy Niavaran, surrounded by sycophants and yes-men in ignorant bliss, the children were outside calling for the downfall of the King of Kings. They shouted until they thought their little lungs would burst, hurled the biggest stones their tiny hands could clutch, and raised their placards high. Bowie had sung of a starman in the sky who'd blow everyone's minds; and, to the children, that starman had a name: Ayatollah Ruhollah Khomeini. Just as their destinies had been scrawled upon their foreheads, still smooth and taut, so had Khomeini's face been hacked onto that of the moon above. *It had all been written* – or so they thought.

The Shah's time, at least in the colourful world of these children, had come to an end. Everywhere, Khomeini's name was being whispered – in classrooms, in clubs, in clandestine meetings reeking of *Eau Sauvage*. On the surface, the heroes of these children sang songs about flowers, pilgrims, and lovers; but everyone knew that something had changed in those voices. It wasn't the same Googoosh, the same Farhad, the same Dariush the kids were hearing; they too, along with the small circle of poets who penned their songs, were sticking it to the Shah, albeit in their own way. Each song and each word began to take on a new meaning. Everything was interpreted as an act of resistance and protest, and, even if the songs were as innocent as poor old Mash Ghasem, the children wanted to *believe* they were laden with innuendo. In the pictures, too, could one see images of foreboding. Parviz Sayyad had lampooned the Shah's '71 celebrations as a massive cock-up (literally), and it seemed it was only a matter of time before they'd see him grimacing above the title, *Samad be Shah Bilakh Migooyad* (*Samad Tells the Shah, 'Up Yours!'*). Badass Behrouz, on the other hand, could still put scores of pimps and thugs to rout, and the children never forgot for a moment that he too was on their side. Ah, if only Gheysar and Shir Mammad had been with them on those bloodied streets, giving the Shah's cronies a taste of their rusty knives – that would have shown 'em! Jubilant, they would have clapped their hands, shining in the most brilliant hues of red beneath the beating sun, and shaken their scrawny hips to that ominous chant and groove: *Marg bar Shah, marg bar Shah, marg bar Shaaah!*

When not out fighting on the streets, they sat with burning ears pressed against transistor radios, waiting with bated breath for news from the palaces. Before long, the day the children and their heroes had long been waiting for arrived: on January 16, 1979, the Shah – the King of Kings, the Light of the Aryans, God's Shadow on Earth – left Iran, never to return. How the children poured into the streets, honking their horns, gyrating on motorbikes, and grinning like madmen, all the while waving around newspapers with those two words, in big bold letters, that would burn themselves into their brains, never to be forgotten: *Shah raft! The Shah left!* And, soon enough, the starman came down from the sky, to blow the children's minds and give them all a surprise.

* * *

They didn't know where it had all gone wrong. Perhaps it really *had* been too good to be true. So much for the oil money and free electricity. So much for Googoosh and the good times they'd taken for granted. Where was *Khanum* Googoosh then? In the streets, darts were being thrown at pictures of Hayedeh, and it was later rumoured that Ramesh, the curly-haired queen of funk, had died. The children's hair stood on their ends as they recalled Dariush's vision of a bleak millennium, which it seemed had already arrived: *the year of dead-ends, of clawing at walls in vain, of spirituality's demise.* They yearned for the breeze of the East to change its course, but knew it was too late; and, though they cursed themselves, their tears fell unheeded and their cries on deaf ears.

No, the sun did not shine above their heads, of the likes of my father and uncle. It was the moment of the wretched, the forgotten, the downtrodden, the broken. Golden locks, forlorn and pallid, were veiled beneath swarthy swathes; in vain had they taken to the streets, marching in their skirts and heels, their hair billowing over their supple shoulders. Like the shroud of the Empire, on which only a faint outline of the Lion and Sun could be made out amidst rags and tatters in deepest red, the children – daughters, sisters, mothers – were wrapped and bound in black. The field of tulips lay barren, its bulbs that once glowed atop promenading playboys and belles cracked and shattered. There would be no more dirty French matinées, no more coffeehouse romps, and no more childhood heroes that burst into all the colours of the rainbow on the television. Filth! Sleaze! Blasphemy!

Uncle Mehrdad was leaning outside his balcony in Tehran, playing with a burning cigarette between his fingers. He remembered how, only months ago, he could hear the sound of schoolgirls laughing on their way home and 6/8 rhythms blasting from orange-coloured taxicabs. Now, he only saw black – *everywhere, black* – and visions of hellfire sparked by ominous-sounding words incanted in an alien tongue. He didn't know that, before too long, from beyond the Khuzestan of childhood days and nights, would rush forth hordes crying, screaming, and howling in that very tongue. Taking a drag on his cigarette, he looked out into the sky, blanketed in clouds, cursing the sun and moon alike.

* * *

Mammad could see the faint outlines of the tanks in the distance. Beneath the hot, throbbing sun lay the mangled remains of his friends and comrades. He couldn't tell who was who; some had been burnt to a cinder, while the faces of others had been cleaved to bits in a burning hailstorm of shrapnel and lead. There, on the other side, Ezrail himself was waiting to take him away from that damned wasteland to the black void of death and nothingness, which he thirsted for then more than ever. Sweat dripped from his crimson headband, on which had been written the hallowed name of Hossein, King of Martyrs. He rubbed his little fingers against it, kissed them, and pressed them to his forehead, invoking the fallen saint of Karbala all the while. He noticed blood on his fingers, but it wasn't his. He wished everyone would stop screaming; he wanted to bury his head in the scorched earth, fill his ears with sand, and think of his mother, his little house with melons floating in the pool outside, and the way Goli, their neighbour's daughter, always blushed when she passed by him in the alley. He could have buried himself alive, just as they'd done to his friends. He envied Peyman, who the day before had sacrificed himself to detonate a landmine; Peyman wasn't there to see what he would forever be unable to *un-*see, at least. *Saddam, you son of a bitch!*

Iran was in shambles, and the bastard of Baghdad had struck while the iron was hot. He'd always had his eyes on Khuzestan, and then had his chance. Together with the other petty dictators of the Arab world, who had all grovelled before the Shah (you used to have such fun water-skiing with him, King Hussein), and, blessed with all the weapons he could ask for by the Americans and European powers, Saddam Hussein vowed to show the *Majus* another Qadissiya. He would make those haughty *Ajams* kneel before his might, and revive the

121

humiliation of the seventh century amongst them and their saturnine saviour. It all seemed too easy; Saddam had the world on his side – how could he lose to a ragtag, beggarly bunch of rabble-rousers with a mullah for their leader?

Mammad had wanted to fight for Iran alongside the big boys, ever since Khomeini first called upon all those able to join the 'imposed' struggle. He didn't care whether he lived to tell the tale or not – that was beside the point; he was only too fain to give his life for Iran and the will of the Imam. Whenever he felt his legs giving in or his tiny heart about to explode, he looked at the picture of Khomeini he always carried in his shirt pocket, recalled the plight of Imam Hossein, and imagined Iran herself standing proudly before him: no, he wouldn't let her be fucked by those Iraqis and left for dead, and her children forget the tongue of lovers, of Paradise.

I have to attack those tanks, he thought to himself. He tightened his headband between his sweaty palms, and joined the throng of scruffy children, their faces roughened by clouds of sand, their eyes wide open, their smooth, small hands ready to grasp and claw at whatever they could catch. They jumped over bushes of fire and light; how different were they than the ones of their childhood, the ones Farhad had sung about! They fell in droves, gunned down by those seemingly invincible Iraqi tanks, those razor-toothed monsters of iron and smoke; but Mammad didn't look back, not even for a second. All he could hear were animal-like wails of '*Khoda!*' and the harrowing trumpet of Ezrail, the Angel of Death. Yes, it was him, all right – there was no mistaking him. He swore by God and the blood of Imam Hossein that he would reach that tank, as if all his blackened days had culminated in that very moment, his hour of truth. His chest was aching, and he feared the ball within would stop pounding before he'd be able to get to it. '*Ya Khoda!*' he cried, '*Ya Hossein!*' as he stretched out his bare hands before him erupting into a blinding, numbing sheet of light.

'Alas, Mammad!' they later lamented. 'You weren't there to see how we reclaimed our city! Our blood was not spilled in vain!' Goli wept when she saw the two soldiers knock on his mother's door in their dusty little alley. They looked at the ground as Mammad's mother dug her nails into her face. 'Accept our congratulations and condolences' were the only words they could say. Her little boy had become a martyr.

* * *

Eight years. Eight goddamn years. Khomeini had drunk from the poisoned chalice and called for an end to a war that had seen the Iraqis run back home with their tails between their legs. Saddam had underestimated the children of the Revolution, they who had nothing but love and faith; but the bloodshed had to end somewhere. Had the Americans no shame, knowingly bombing a civilian aeroplane full of women and children and not even bothering to apologise? Were Iranian children the only ones they could pick on? The Iranians were advancing well into Iraq, but withdrew at the will of the Imam. Iran was free again, and all throughout the land of the noble, the children wept tears of joy and sorrow for their fallen brothers and sisters, from whose blood sprouted tulips, and under whose shadows they walked the city streets.

The war was over, and, in less than a year, only the memory of Khomeini would remain. It seemed the children had seen it all and been through the worst: revolution, civil strife, war, isolation, economic turmoil. They had thought things couldn't get any worse under the rule of the Shah, yet they *had* gotten worse – *much* worse. How would they pick up the pieces? Where was their place in society? Where were the heroes and idols of yesteryear – Khomeini, Behrouz, the Shah? No, they didn't even have a Shah to hit them in the head and show them the way, right or wrong. How could they be fathers and mothers when they themselves didn't know what was happening around them? Many had stayed, but many had gone long before, to the land of the Franks and of milk and honey; and, though the war had ended, the spirit of the dead haunted the children yet. The names of the streets, the murals on the walls, the images on the television, the hazy studio pictures with black bands and newly sprouted moustaches – everything in Iran served as a mirror for those fallen cherubs, the living dead.

It was a time for the departed, but also the living. Heirs of the days of blood and fire, the seedlings of a new generation had blossomed along with the tulips of the pure. The faces of the Shah and Farah had been effaced from their schoolbooks, now adorned with flowers and youth brimming with revolutionary zeal chanting, 'Independence! Freedom! The Islamic Republic!' Daddy was still baking bread, and Sa'di still delivering his sermons; but the floodgates had opened, and the saints had come marching in. The children were taught to be like Kobra, Zaynab, and other models of Islamic piety and righteousness who bit their tongues on bended knee. They read not about Mohammad Reza Shah Pahlavi, but Zahhak, the demon-king himself, who with the twain serpents slithering atop his shoulders, fed on the brains of men. The Revolution, after all, had to be defended, and its children – the new generation – were seen as the future guardians of all the Imam had deemed holy.

Like their parents, the children led double lives in public and behind closed doors. They too were bearing the brunt of sanctions and damnation on their tiny shoulders, and, with their imagination and undaunted spirits, had to create something out of nothing in their own private Iran. But the times,

they were a-changin'; soon came a smiling chap
named Khatami, and new-fangled things called
mahvareh and *Eenternet*. Slowly, as if they were
discovering other planets, the children began to
realise that they weren't alone. There were leggy
blondes in America with strawberry highlights,
prettier than even Fatemeh Mo'tamed-Arya. There
were European arthouse films, new and old, to be
gorged upon and understood. There was a world
outside of Iran, and they wanted, with all their
heart, to be a part of it.

Freedom, the children soon learned, tasted good; at
long last, the little ones had a reason to fight! Ali
Kuchulu was all grown up, and they would all
fight, just as their parents and the fallen ones had –
for freedom, *sweet freedom*, and what they thought
was rightfully theirs. Again, those bloodied palms,
those banners stained red, those black bands. Over
and over would the sound of gunshots and slogans
echo down the back alleys of Pahlavi – nay, *Vali-ye
Asr* – Avenue, and the blood of children stream
down the streets, following the course of the cool
water from the towering mountains beyond. They
would daub their hands and faces in red and green,
and, like Mister Jimi, wave their freak flags high.
They would be cut down, crushed beneath black
leather boots, and branded as thuggish enemies of
the state; but always, from side-streets and
mountain crevices alike, would resound a cry
familiar to one and all: the cry of them, the
children of the Revolution.

They tried to rob them of their language, culture, and very identity. They tried to efface their glory from the annals of history, and bury it along with their ruins beneath the stained earth of Khorasan and the plains of Persepolis. They tried to revive amongst them the memory of Qadissiya, and make widowers of their women and bastards of their sons. They tried to silence their voices, quash their desires, and, blacken their names. But throughout the centuries, throughout incendiary days of embers and tulips dripping with the tears of the bereaved and the dew of dawn, there was one thing they could not snatch away from their scarred young hands: hope, the purest hope, draped in red, white, and green, shining as brightly as the sun.

* * *

The ticking of the clock, the scent of hyacinths, the thought of those gone, and those who will soon be. Uncle Mehrdad in his cigarette carton suit, Farhad strumming his steel-string guitar with closed eyes, Maman Aziz sweeping the house in the ungodly hours of the morning, and the faces – a million different faces – of those above and below the cool earth, and their pure blood: the blood of flowers, the blood of the noble. I hadn't been there, and had no memories to call my own; there was only a story to read, of Iran, a million miles away, and her glorious children, *whose blood has not been spilled in vain.*

Joobin Bekhrad

Because of you, children of the Revolution, has
our winter come to an end.

4/5/2016

*In memory of Mehrdad Bekhrad (1951 – 1997) and the
martyrs of the Iran-Iraq War (1980 – 1988).*

Ramblings of an Iranian Wino

I was at that little hole in the wall again, as usual. I winced at the sensation of cool droplets trickling down my back and sides, yet didn't doff my tweed blazer or the green scarf tossed around my neck in a beggarly fashion; somehow, they seemed to complement the mood of the evening. If you listened hard enough, you could hear, amongst the clanking of bottles and boorish banter, the Kinks playing on the stereo. I wondered then why I'd never once said hello to Ray Davies out of all the times I'd stumbled upon him on Highgate Hill. 'Who's that?' one of my mates would say, noticing me starting at someone in the corner of The Flask. 'Ah, just some rock and roller … you wouldn't know.' But there wasn't anyone with me that night; scrunched up in a corner booth, my only companions were a fast-diminishing glass of cheap red wine and an old puce hardback I'd brought along to read by candlelight. I had eaten very little that day, and was already feeling those first warm rushes to the head. The guitars had become dirtier, and Davies' words clearer. I had yet again found myself upon that sublime threshold of the senses, where I would, but for a moment, behold myself – *remember* myself – as I really was. *Hah! I gave birth to my father!* I thought with a wide, smarting grin. Not having the slightest ability to trudge onwards through the paragraphs ahead, I simply played with the book in my hands, flipping to the page opposite the one I'd recently finished reading. Again, a smile, this time accentuated by the levity of my knees. Holding the book closer to the candle, I read a passage:

> The people were a laughing, careless set, devoid of fanaticism, having indeed very little religion. Nearly all drank wine to excess. The women seldom veiled, and talked with me without any 'mauvaise-honte'.[1]

Oh, how I longed for my Iran then. Smudging the smooth page with my bony fingers, I resigned myself to the whims of the daughter of the vine. Watching her essence tumble back and forth in my glass, it took on a new shade and tinge. *An old friend*, I thought, relishing her notes on my tongue. That ruddy elixir was my birthright as an Iranian; I was no mere bacchant. I had been baptised with fire and wine – yea, it had long coursed through my veins. My Lord, Wisdom, my lifeblood, wine. In blood and wine is the history of my ancient homeland steeped; and I, as a child of Iran, am a proud wino. Why feel any shame or deny the fact? To do so would be base hypocrisy and artifice. As once asked Baudelaire, 'Isn't it reasonable to think that men who never drink wine, whether out of naivety or on principle, are imbeciles or hypocrites?' Truly, 'A man who drinks only water has a secret to hide from his fellow men'[2]. If the

Romans found truth in wine, I have also found in it the soul of my people.

* * *

Long before my Aryan forebears descended upon my land had the pure earth of my homeland been awash with the blood of grapes. Indeed, the stained tongues of the ancient Elamites and those who had come before them knew well the hidden pleasures of the vine, and it is in their vanquished realm that our story begins. The oldest known traces of grape wine – dating back some seven thousand-odd years – were found in the Zagros mountain range of western Iran[3]. Who knows to which love songs my progenitors drank their draughts, to the strains of which lutes? Proudly they ruled, until condemned to dust by the vicissitudes of time. Those people of the mountains at times appear in my mind as the objects they fashioned of stone and clay; cold, lifeless, and inhuman. But why? For *tomorrow, when from this ancient realm we depart, shall we be just like those seven thousand years old*[4].

Along with the Aryan tribesmen from afar had come a prophet, enrobed in white, his gaze ever directed towards the empyrean. I can see him standing proudly before King Vishtaspa, his *Gathas* in one hand and a flagon in the other. With the wine given him by the hallowed Zarathustra, Vishtaspa beheld the glory of Ahura Mazda (God) and the *Amesha Spentas*[5]. Similarly, it was by way of a concoction of wine and a narcotic mixed in three golden goblets that Arda Viraf, that cosmic traveller, journeyed to the burning fires of Hell and Mazda's House of Song[6]. It would not be for divine revelation, however, but something very different that the purple-robed Persian heirs of the Prophet would later quaff heavenly draughts in their courts.

The might and magnanimity of Cyrus the Great had given rise to the largest empire the world had ever witnessed. The deeds of our illustrious 'Father' and the immanent qualities that so elevated him to his exalted position have been extolled by Iranians and non-Iranians alike. In the Old Testament, Cyrus appears as a messiah on account of his liberation of the Jews from Babylon[7]. Likewise, Xenophon – though bearing an understandable bitterness towards the Persians, as any Greek mercenary would have naturally bore – presented Cyrus as the ruler *par excellence* towards which all must aspire[8]. Centuries later in another 'mirror for princes', Niccolò Machiavelli, in making a reference to Xenophon's *Cyropaedia*, also praised Cyrus as a paragon of leadership. 'Whoever reads the [*Cyropaedia*] will recognise afterwards in the life of Scipio how that imitation was his glory,' he wrote, 'and how in chastity, affability, humanity, and liberality Scipio conformed to those things which have been written of Cyrus by Xenophon'[9]. Aeschylus, too, venerated

Cyrus, 'blessed of men, who, as he ruled, established peace for all his friends … God did not begrudge his rule, so wise was he'[10].

In their deliberations and debates, though, were the rulers of Iran and *Aniran* simply looking to follow the example that had been set for them by the one who had catapulted them to greatness? Herodotus – another 'father', this time of history – praised Cyrus in expounding on the ways of the Persians, although he also recorded something novel about the decision-makers of the age. According to him, the Persians would customarily discuss and argue over the 'gravest matters' not when they were of sound mettle, but rather when they'd had one too many cups of the good stuff. Afterwards, when they'd sobered up, they would revisit the issues of the previous evening, and accept their initial decisions only if they agreed with them again. The opposite was also true: 'And if they have deliberated about a matter when sober,' wrote the Father of History, 'they decide upon it when they are drunk'[11]. And so, it was not only with Zarathustra's idea of 'good thoughts, good words, and good deeds' that a realm stretching from Greece to India was governed, but also good drinks.

It was perhaps amidst spilled rhytons and tumblers that Alexander forced his way into Darius' palace in Persepolis and razed it – along with its libraries – to the ground. Some, like Diodorus, have said that

Aristotle's ambitious pupil had been drunk at the time[12], and later repented having committed such a deed[13]. The idea of a sloshed Alexander is not difficult to digest, especially considering his attitudes towards the Persians. While he had been compelled by an ambition to crush the seemingly indomitable Achaemenid Empire as a fair-haired child, his desire was arguably a mixture of hatred and awe; for not only did Alexander honour the fallen Darius III upon his death (at the hands of two Persian soldiers, whom he swiftly executed on account of their insolence), but also took Persian wives for himself and his generals, and quickly began imitating the ways of the Persian emperors, much to the dismay of his followers[14]. Thus, while wine may have fuelled the Persian Empire during the Achaemenid centuries, it might have also led to the destruction of that fruit of the genius of Persian architecture and opulence: Persepolis, the Persian City.

* * *

> Behold, O heart! Look before thee – pay heed,
> And Khosrow's Arch of Ctesiphon a lesson deem!
> … Thou wouldst say the Tigris wept a hundred bloody more,
> That from its lashes warm with blood, fire didst pour.
> – Khaghani Shirvani (d. 1190 AD)[16]

Alas! In the wake of the Arab armies that followed in the footsteps of the Greeks, the palaces of Ctesiphon and Istakhr resounded with the howls of spirits and crows. The place where Khosrow had once reclined on velvet cushions, lending an ear to the strains of Barbad's *barbat* and sipping on thick wine, had become but a heap of ruins, roughened cairns in memory of Cyrus' children laid low. The Abbasids, upon their arrival in Iran, were quick to inherit the Persian notion of court culture and the various traditions (e.g. literary and musical) associated with it. 'A complete model of imperial rule was thus presented to the Arabs by the Persian realm,' wrote the late Iranologist Richard Nelson Frye, 'and the Arabs borrowed more from Sassanian Iran than any other source'[16]. During the reign of the storied Haroun al Rashid (born in the ancient city of Rey near Tehran[17]), the poetry and wit of his boon companion Abu Nuwas became renowned in Baghdad and beyond. Staying true to his half-Persian roots, the verses of Nuwas were laden with explicit references to wine and drunken revelry[18]. Nuwas, however, as a client of the Abbasids, wrote exclusively in Arabic; it was not until the Samanids of northeast Iran came along in the ninth century that the prominence of wine in the psyche and culture of Iranians was again asserted in Persian, in spite of all religious proscriptions[19]. That's not to say that the Samanids were the only sots of their times, though; far from it. A saucy passage from the otherwise sterile *Tarikh-e Beyhaghi* (*History of Beyhaghi*) paints a somewhat different picture during the Ghaznavid epoch. Concerning the escapades of the wayward prince Amir Mas'ud, Beyhaghi wrote:

> ...When [Amir Mas'ud] was living in Herat, he used to drink wine without his father's knowledge, and unbeknown to the eunuch Reyhan, he used to arrange intimate sessions in the cellars of the palace and have musicians and singers, both male and female, brought to him through secret ways ... They decorated this summer-house, from ceiling to floor, with pictures from the book called *Alfiyya*, depicting different ways of intercourse between men and women, all of them naked, so that the whole book with its stories was illustrated there; and apart from these, they painted other pictures in the same manner. The Amir used to go there at siesta time and would sleep there. It is a mark of young men that they do this and similar things.[20]

During the renaissance ushered in by the nationalist Samanids after the 'Two Centuries of Silence' – wherein Iranian (or, *Ajam*, as the ethnicity was derogatorily referred to in Arabic) identity and the Persian language were forcibly suppressed by Iran's invaders[21] – poets such as Rudaki, Daqiqi, and Ferdowsi found patronage and flourished. Widely known as the first noteworthy poet to write in Persian following the fall of the Sassanian Empire[22], Rudaki's poetry in many ways adumbrated that of the giants who would succeed him, and was, of course, replete with celebrations of wine. In one of the extant poems in his *Divan*, he wrote (or sang, rather):

> *Wine giveth rise to honour in man;*
> *Divide the freeborn from the slave it can.*
> *Many a merit within doth wine contain;*
> *Whenever one drinketh it, they happiness attain.*[23]

So too did Daqiqi – who fared no better, perhaps, than Rudaki, who was accused of being an Isma'ili heretic and left to ignominiously die as a blind man[24] – eulogise wine, as he did the Zoroastrian faith of his ancestors, to which Rudaki had also made overt allusions. *Four things are there dear, which I so need,* Daqiqi wrote, *more than all the world's pleasures and beauties indeed.* His list came in true Iranian fashion, one could say: *the ruby-coloured lip, the harp's lament, the blood-red wine, and Zarathustra's creed*[25]. Not surprisingly, Daqiqi paid for his brazenness with his life, leaving Ferdowsi to pick up the pieces and finish the monumental work in honour of Iran that he'd only just begun: the *Khodai Nameh*, which was later realised as the *Shahnameh*[26]. If only like Damghani, Daqiqi, had you had longed for less! The man was happy with but *sharab* (wine), kebab, and the *robab*[27].

* * *

As I thumbed the creamy pages of my book, not so much reading their words as gazing at little blotches of ink, I remembered another friend. I had first become acquainted with him in an unassuming café in Crouch End, when the down on my cheek was still smooth and my trousers didn't fit properly. Reading his verses, I imagined a hoary old man reclining in a hovel, etching profundities on parchment, and waiting – always waiting – for the cupbearer to bring him his fill. I could even picture him kneeling down as he cupped his earthen bowl with palms outstretched, looking at the vessel before him and wondering from the dust of whose beloved it might have been moulded. His words, soaked in wine, were sobering for one drunk on the thought of better things to come, and haunting. Like the camel of death that sleeps at everyone's doorstep, Omar Khayyam's words seemed to cling to me more tenaciously than even the scrawny little shadow I cast. 'So what do you think of Khayyam's poems, *baba*?' asked my father, after I'd rung him up outside the 12 Bar Club one afternoon. 'I'm depressed.'

Perhaps, as with wine, I needed to give Khayyam's philosophies a bit of time to mature in my mind before being able to fully appreciate them. As I came, slowly, to shatter the fetters I'd bound myself during the age of ignorance called 'childhood', Khayyam's wine appeared clearer and clearer to me. Looking out at the little alley outside the pub window, naked beneath the revelations of bright white streetlamps, I recalled our long nights together pondering the mysteries of existence and the virtues of the vine. Khayyam! Had I had my grandfather's little Mini, I'd have run twenty red lights in your honour; but sadly, I had only the sweet ichor swirling about in my head and dwindling glass. I drank whatever I had in memory of the greatest Iranian wino there had ever been and would ever be, and slowly made my way through the suited throng to the bar to ask for more. 'Yeah, I'll have another glass of the Shiraz …' What a moment it had been, when, walking down Hampstead Hill in the full bloom of spring, Shamlou whispered those verses in my ear:

> *Bereft of pure wine, can I live not;*
> *Without it, this body's weight can I carry not.*
> *I'm a slave to that moment the cup-bearer whispers,*
> *'Have another glass', and I cannot.*[27]

In vino veritas! And though I did not recall dear Hafez in my drunken hour, his image appears before me now. Lover, sinner, saint – all have tried to label you in vain. As Khayyam would have said, *I myself is what I am*[28]. In all your complexities and contradictions, you embodied the human condition; and – you clever rogue – you also enjoyed a nice stiff drink every now and then. Hafez, lurking in the shadows of Shiraz's taverns, downing flask after flask of choice Khollar wine, waiting for inspiration whilst enraptured by a Turk. In Zarathustra's children, you found friends and confidantes, and in the Magian Elder, a guide. With them, it seemed you had found yourself and forgotten all you had been forced to commit to

Joobin Bekhrad

memory. *Sick am I of the hypocrite's cloak and his shrine,* you once uttered, likely in a paroxysm of passion. *Where is the Magian temple and its pure wine?*[29] Knowing well the fate of poor Daqiqi, you spoke in riddles, confusing the bloody hell out of your admirers and detractors alike, including a teenage me; but, in doing so, you kept your head and ensured your children would, too. Hafez, how well have you taught them. Today, scholars rack their brains trying to figure you out; hell, they've even given their obsession a name: *Hafez-Shenasi.* I wonder if they've ever had their head reeling with the 'metaphorical' wine you so adored, and which held no secrets from you. I know well the words of a wino, of the brethren of the bottle. Tonight (for my head is still spinning from last night's draught on this September's morn) shall I don the ring of the Magi, and, with my tongue stained purple, flip to a page of your dripping *Divan* to see what the stars have set aside for me. Goethe's ambition is mine, as mine was his: *Hafiz … To love like thee, like thee to drink, shall be my pride, shall be my life*[30].

* * *

I have been rambling on for ages, but am still stuck in the fourteenth century! What can I say? Wine maketh quick the passing of time. I have yet to tell you about another Persian renaissance, another golden age drowned in waves of blood-red wine; for, as said the poet, *If I do not make merry now, then when shall I?*[31] Truly, as much as the Safavids loved the arts and fought to defend (and expand) Iran's borders to the teeth, they fancied getting plastered. In his travelogue, the Italian pilgrim Pietro Della Valle remarked of having partook in a round of wine drinking in the presence of Shah Abbas the Great, that august monarch so lauded by Maraghe'i's nationalist protagonist in *The Travel Diary of Ebrahim Beg*[32]. Although Della Valle didn't particularly enjoy the Persian varieties of wine he had been treated to[33], Shah Abbas certainly seemed to have had a rather good time. A contemporary of Della Valle's – the French jeweller-cum-English aristocrat John Chardin – also made similar observations of the King of Kings. '… The King being in a Debauch, and as drunk as it was possible to be', wrote he, 'caus'd some Wine to be presented to the Grand Vizier'. But the Grand Vizier didn't want a drink; as Baudelaire would not have, Shah Abbas did not approve of the fellow, either. 'The King seeing his Obstinacy, bid the Cup-bearer fling the Wine in his Face … the King … looking at him with a jeering Air, told him; Grand Vizier, I can no longer bear, that thou shouldst here preserve thy Senses, while we are all drunk.'[34] Teetotallers were not, evidently, favoured in the court of the Great Sophy.

Chardin's account of Persian drunkenness and debauchery was far from being limited to only Shah Abbas and his retinue, though. In the eyes of the jeweller, Iranians were – contrary to popular expectations of pious 'Mussulmans' and

Joobin Bekhrad

'Mahometans' – a nation of drunkards. An anthropologist and linguist he may not have been (his travelogue is rife with egregious statements and inaccuracies), but he knew a lush when he saw one:

> Wine and intoxicating Liquors are forbid the Mahometans; yet, there is scarce any one who does not drink of some sort of strong Liquor. The Courtiers, Gentlemen, and Rakes, drink Wine, and as they all use it, as a Remedy against Sorrow, and that one Part drink it to put them to Sleep, and the other to warm and make them Merry; they generally drink the Strongest, and most Heady, and if this does not make them presently Drunk, they say 'what Wine is this?'[35]

* * *

It's almost noon, and the bottle is beckoning. I know, however, that if I open that bottle of chardonnay teasing me in the corner of my eye, I'll never be able to finish our tale. Am I, in the eyes of some, destined for Hell? Perhaps. But, wine aside, my list of sins is a long one. Better then, one might recommend, to follow the advice of another northern soul like myself. Did Keikavus' son live by the lessons he had so eloquently committed to writing for him? Who knows. 'If you drink wine, let it be the finest', he exhorted to Gilanshah in his *Qabus Nameh* (*Book of Qabus*), 'if you listen to music let it be the sweetest, and if you commit a forbidden act, let it be with a beautiful partner'. Been there, done that; but why? 'So that even though you may be convicted of sin in the next world, you will at any rate not be branded a fool in this.'[36] It seems I am finally living up to my name; a wino I may be, but certainly no fool!

Considering the descriptions of European travellers such as Chardin and the frescoes of the Chehel Sotoon (Forty Columns) palace the Qajar prince Zell-ol-Soltan so essayed to cover up with plaster[37], can there be any doubt that the Safavids, too, were People of the Bottle? 'If we can judge by the quantity of wine vessels placed before the guests [in the Safavid-era frescoes], hard drinking seems in their time to have been the order of the day', wrote James Ussher in *A Journey from London to Persepolis*[38]. If the faded Safavids of Chehel Sotoon fame were to Ussher but 'half-drunken revellers', the Qajars – who would seize the imperial throne in the wake of the Afghan sacking of Esfahan and the tribal chaos that ensued after the crumbling of Nader Shah's short-lived empire – were full-blown winos (and rock and rollers, to boot). The mere thought of them is sending my mind into a flurry, but I will resist the temptation (for now) to pull out that sweet-smelling cork. As the Qajars sucked dry the blood of my people, so too did they the blood of grapes. Would that I could banish such troubling thoughts, and, like Morier's fabled Hajji Baba and his beloved Zeenab, simply enjoy my

wine, guitar, and the poems of that master tippler,
Hafez! '… We did and felt as if all that surrounded
us was our own, and that the wine and our love
would last forever,' remembered the *Hajji*. 'Having
sang several more songs and emptied several cups
of wine,' he continued, 'I found that my poetry was
exhausted as well as our bottle'[39]. But no, the
images are appearing as vividly as ever now: bodies
walled up by the roadside; bedraggled pariahs and
lepers traipsing through lonely alleyways; slit wrists
in a Kerman bathhouse; and above all, Iran,
humiliated and sold like a cheap whore to all and
sundry. *All washed in wine, the nectar of the gods …*

* * *

There I was, half-drunk in the candle's glow,
thinking the brothers Davies right badasses, having
forgotten all about the legacy of sex, drugs, and *gol-
o-bolbol* left by the Qajars. Though Western
travelogues concerning Qajar-era Iran read more
like tragedies than anything else (as Maraghe'i
would have likely agreed), peppered throughout
them are juicy anecdotes of not only binge
drinking, but also extravagant depravity in general.
Even a toper, dear reader, has their principles. A
wino is a wino – that is that; but not all winos,
mind you, are created equal. And with this thought
in mind, we shall now approach the zenith of
Iranian drunkenness and debauchery, the
sumptuous fruit of our morning's labours!

After trekking through the torrid, burning deserts of Syria and Iraq, the redoubtable English explorer Sir Henry Austen Layard set his charred feet on the wine-drenched soil of fair Persia. Considering his account of an episode in Esfahan, it seems the Persians had yet to give up their ancient ways; old habits, after all, die hard. At the house of some nobleman or other (I fail to remember exactly whose), Layard witnessed a rather striking display of profligacy – striking to he, of course, who had not been initiated into our boozy Persian rites:

> The musicians were women who played on guitars and dulcimers. These orgies usually ended by the guests getting very drunk, and falling asleep on their carpets, where they remained until sufficiently sober to return to their homes in the morning.[40]

If that isn't rock and roll, then I don't know what is. To top things off (or, rather, to take the top off things), Layard's Qajar beauties were minimalists when it came to fashion: 'Their costume consisted of loose silk jackets of some gay colour, entirely open in front so as to show the naked figure to the waist'[41]. Indeed, we had our ya-yas out, kicking out the jams like it was nobody's business centuries ago. In Layard's time, as in Wills', bacchanalia was still very much in vogue and the 'order of the day'. When Wills went to visit a patient at around ten pm one evening, he noticed a slight change of atmosphere. 'The same stifling room, the same hard drinking, only now *everybody* was drinking', he was quick to observe. 'Dancing-boys and singers, shrieking the noisy love-songs of Persia in chorus, were keeping up the spirits of my patient.' In Wills' Iran, fruit gardens were 'merely a good place to get drunk in', and mullahs – though 'mostly at heart freethinkers ... Deists ... [and] Atheists', there being 'very few good Mussulmans' – were avid oenophiles who would not even begrudge infidels the secrets of their practice. 'I was considerably amused at the [mullah] actually carrying on the art of winemaking and instructing the unbeliever', wrote Wills[42]. To an Iranian, however, it most probably would have been just an ordinary day in Persia.

Like their Iranic cousins the Persians, the Kurds were no different when it came to dissolution. Much of the opulence and *joie de vivre* of the Persians, had, after all, been passed down to them by the Medes[43], another Aryan tribe that had ruled Iran before the rise of Cyrus the Great. An account of the Kurdish *Ilkhan* of Ghoochan in northeast Iran (blessed be the winos of Khorasan!) takes the cake and makes all other such passages pale in comparison. In the late nineteenth century, the Russian colonel Nikolai Ivanovich Groedekoff visited the residence of the *Ilkhan*, who seemingly left our Russian friend in awe:

Knowing that [the Ilkhan] was fond of liquor, we placed several bottles of wine, liqueurs, and vodka before him; and in a very short time the Shuja had drunk several glasses of different wines, and then called in his singers and musicians. The men who came with him, his surgeon, and his favourites, Vali Khan and Ramzan Khan, drank themselves stupid, and a regular orgy began. Next day I went to see the Amir, and presented my documents to him. Bottles were already standing before him, and he explained that he was recovering from his intoxication. During our conversation he repeatedly partook of brandy, opium, hashish, and wine, and by noon was quite drunk. In the evening of the same day he invited us to a European supper, and again got intoxicated to the last degree.[44]

Tom Waits' notion of a bad idea is trying to outdrink Keith Richards. 'Don't you ever, ever do that', he once said[45]. It's a good thing, perhaps, that the two never had the chance to cross paths with the inebriated *Ilkhan*.

* * *

But enough for now – the bottle beckons, that dear old friend. At gatherings, I can't help but cringe when I hear an old curmudgeon whine to some

Englishman or other, 'Of course I *dee-reenk!* When the Shah was around, *ever-ee-body* used to!' When the Shah was around? Honey, we hail from a culture of drunks – we were suckled on grapes! No, it is not *my* doing – this love of wine is something in my blood; in crimson hues was my destiny scrawled upon my brow. It is my heritage, one of the many blessings that have been passed down to me by my noble forebears. If I am to be judged, so be it; and if Hell be my lot? As said the sage, *Should lovers and drunkards to hellfire be damned, Heaven tomorrow shall be like an empty hand*[46]. Nay, I worry not for the company I will soon come to keep.

As an Iranian, I find in wine Paradise, damnation, and the shining sparks of Mazda. With it, I forget the ravages of the ages and the rape of Iran. I drink so that before my dust becomes the clay of another's chalice, I may savour whatever little is left of this life. With wine, love becomes clear, as does the mirror of my heart; and yes, I also drink because, as an Iranian, I am a natural born *bon viveur* always looking for a good time. Deny me not what is mine! My people, born of fire and smeared with blood, are verily the children of the vine. If it is your pleasure, it is my very essence; but I have again spoken too much when I promised to stop. Come – do you expect me to finish this bottle all by myself? In the words of the great moustachioed Sophy, 'A drunken Man, and a Man that does not drink do not pass their Time very agreeably together'[47].

Here ends our prattle. It is to your health, dear reader, that I shall drink this draught. *Be tandorostiye shoma …*

9/13/2016

Poetry translations by the author.

Bibliography

1. Wills, C.J. *In the Land of the Lion and Sun.* Odenton: Mage, 2004.
2. Baudelaire, C., Drabble, M., trans. *On Wine and Hashish.* London: Hesperus Press, 2002.
3. Wilford, J.N. *For Wine, 5000 B.C. Was Quite a Year.* [online]. 1996. [Accessed 4 September 2016]. Available from: http://www.nytimes. com/ 1996/06/06/us/for-wine-5000-bc-was-quite-a-year.html.
4. Bekhrad, J. *The Quatrains of Omar Khayyam.* Bloomington: Balboa Press, 2017.
5. Russell, G. *Heirs to Forgotten Kingdoms: Journeys into the Disappearing Religions of the Middle East.* New York City: Basic Books, 2014.
6. Horne, C.F., ed. *The Sacred Books and Early Literature of the East, Volume VII: Ancient Persia.* London: Parke, Austin, and Lipscomb Inc., 1917.
7. Norton, D., ed. *The Bible.* London: Penguin, 2006.
8. Xenophon, Ambler, W., trans. *The Education of Cyrus.* Ithaca: Cornell University Press, 2001.

9. Machiavelli, N., Bull, G., trans. *The Prince.* London: Penguin, 2005.

10. Aeschylus, Podlecki, A.J., trans. *Persians.* Bristol: Bristol Classical Press, 1991.

11. Herodotus, Waterfield, R., trans. *The Histories.* New York City: Oxford University Press, 2008.

12. Carlsen, J. *Alexander the Great: Reality and Myth.* Rome: L'Erma de Brechsteider, 1997.

13. Savill, A. *Alexander the Great and His Time.* New York City: Barnes and Noble Books, 1993.

14. Briant, P. *Alexander the Great: The Heroic Ideal.* London: Thames & Hudson, 1996.

15. Ganjoor.net. *Hengam-e Oboor az Madain va Didan-e Tagh-e Kasra* [online]. Accessed 1 September 2016. Available from: http:// ganjoor.net/ khaghani/divankh/ghasidekh/sh168/.

16. Frye, R.N. in Molavi, A. *The Soul of Iran: A Nation's Struggle for Freedom.* New York City: WW Norton, 2005.

17. Christensen, P. *The Decline of Iranshahr: Irrigation and Environments in the History of the Middle East 500 B.C. to A.D. 1500.* Copenhagen: Museum Tusculanum Press, 1993.

18. Irwin, R. *The Penguin Anthology of Classical Arabic Literature.* London: Penguin, 2006.

19. Sykes, E.C. *Persia and its People.* Abingdon: Routledge, 2011.

20. Abu'l-Fazl Beyhaqi, Ashtiany, M., ed., Bosworth, C.E., trans. *The History of Beyhaqi: The History of Sultan Mas'ud of Ghazna, 1030 – 1041, Volume 1.* Boston: Ilex Foundation and the Center

for Hellenic Studies, Trustees for Harvard University, 2011.

21. Taheri, A. *The Persian Night: Iran Under the Khomeinist Revolution*. New York City: Encounter Books, 2009.

22. Tabatabai, S. *Father of Persian Verse: Rudaki and His Poetry*. Leiden: Leiden University Press, 2011.

23. Ibid.

24. Ibid.

25. Starr, Frederick S. *Lost Enlightenment: Central Asia's Golden Age from the Arab Conquest to Tamerlane*. Princeton: Princeton University Press, 2013.

26. Clinton, J.W. *Divan of Manuchihri Damghani: A Critical Study*. Minneapolis: Bibliotheca Islamica, 1972.

27. Bekhrad, J. *The Quatrains of Omar Khayyam*. Bloomington: Balboa Press, 2017.

28. Ibid.

29. Ganjoor.net. *The Ghazals of Hafez – Ghazal #2* [online]. Accessed 1 September 2016. Available from: http://ganjoor.net/hafez/ghazal/ sh2/.

30. Goethe, J.W.V., Bidney, M., trans. *West-East Divan*. Albany: State University of New York Press, 2010.

31. Bekhrad, J. *The Quatrains of Omar Khayyam*. Bloomington: Balboa Press, 2017.

32. Maraghe'i, Z.A., Clark, J.D., trans. *The Travel Diary of Ebrahim Beg*. Santa Ana: Mazda Publishers, 2006.

33. Della Valle, P., Bull, G., trans. *The Pilgrim: The Travels of Pietro Della Valle*. London: Random House, 1989.

34. Chardin, Sir J. *Travels in Persia 1673 – 1677.* Mineola: Dover, 1988.

35. Ibid.

36. Kai Ka'us ibn Iskandar, Levy, R., trans. *A Mirror for Princes: The Qabus Nama.* London: The Cresset Press, 1951.

37. Savory, R. *Iran Under the Safavids.* Cambridge: Cambridge University Press, 1980.

38. Ussher, J. *A Journey from London to Persepolis: Including Wanderings in Daghestan, Georgia, Armenia, Kurdistan, Mesopotamia, and Persia.* London: Hurst and Blackett, 1865.

39. Morier, J.J. *The Adventures of Hajji Baba of Ispahan.* London: The Cresset Press, 1949.

40. Layard, Sir H.A. *Early Adventures in Persia, Susiana, and Babylonia, Including a Residence Among the Bakhtiyari and Other Wild Tribes Before the Discovery of Nineveh.* London: John Murray, 1887.

41. Ibid.

42. Wills, C.J. *In the Land of the Lion and Sun.* Odenton: Mage, 2004.

43. Xenophon, Ambler, W., trans. *The Education of Cyrus.* Ithaca: Cornell University Press, 2001.

44. Curzon, G.N., King, P., ed. *Curzon's Persia.* London: Sidgwick and Jackson, 1988.

45. Keith Richards: Under the Influence [film]. Directed by Morgan Neville. Scotts Valley: Netflix, 2015.

46. Bekhrad, J. *The Quatrains of Omar Khayyam.* Bloomington: Balboa Press, 2017.

47. Chardin, Sir J. *Travels in Persia 1673 – 1677.* Mineola: Dover, 1988.

Of Bandits and Popinjays

My clothes were sticking to me; it had been one hell of a summer's day. I can vaguely recall the hot, viscid bodies on the streets, draped in blue, and the kohl-rimmed eyes of *gamelan* singers obscured by the sun. In the back of a black taxicab, my feet felt as if they were about to burst out of all that smooth leather, and I sensed a familiar light, one of childhood years up north, seep in through the windows. *Performance* was playing that evening, in some stuffy hole in the wall; more hot, viscid bodies, more kohl-rimmed eyes. *Let's have a look!* Through diaphanous tapestries I descried tumbling figures being kissed and bitten, to the ringing sounds of the *santur* and the language of the birds, naked alabaster flesh rubbing against the soft knots of Persian rugs, and frankincense smoke arising from behind a gilded Qajar-era mirror. From Jagger's pouty lips debouched the tale of the Old Man of the Mountain, the gatekeeper of Paradise up high in the crags of Alamut, and, from a little stereoscope, brightly coloured images of *Puhhshia*. 'But I don't want to go to America,' protested the gamine Lucy from beneath silken sheets, 'I wish to be a bandit in Persia'[1]. If my linen shirt had thitherto been sticky, it was now wet. I never found out if Lucy, Pherber, and Turner eventually made it there; amongst the three, perhaps only Chas, the one on the run, attained the object of his desire.

'Gone to Persia', read the blue ink of the brusque note he tossed on his bed.

Outside, I asked myself how I was going to get home, whether or not I should wolf down a falafel sandwich, and where on earth that film had been all my life.

* * *

Reading about the exploits of my rock and roll heroes as a peach fuzz-sporting schoolboy, I would often come across the names of 'exotic' environs such as India and Morocco – but never Iran, or anywhere else in the Iranic world. I didn't make much of it, or feel compelled to dig my fingers into any dusty tomes to stumble upon lost chapters of rock and roll history. To me, Iran and rock and roll – and anything else good and wholesome, for that matter – were mutually exclusive, and incompatible. Iran was a 'dangerous' country; there were no rock and roll stars there, nor had any ever hailed from it. If anything, Iran was the very antithesis of rock and roll, a fearsome stretch of land bridging magical India and civilised Europe, in close proximity to the equally threatening Arab world. The Beatles had gone to India, and the Stones, both in the sixties as well as the eighties, to Morocco. Page and Plant had also travelled to Morocco, and had even been inspired to write a song in the Saharan Desert, albeit one about faraway Kashmir[2]. I associated the *sitar* not with its

Persian namesake (it literally means 'three strings', and refers to the three-stringed Persian instrument of the same name) or any gurus of classical Indian music, but rather, George Harrison, Brian Jones, and the psychedelia of the late sixties. I had even thought that the paisley pattern was of Indian origin; after all, nothing Iranian could have been in vogue then, could it? Seldom did I come across the terms 'Iranian' and 'Persian' in my readings, particularly the former; but why? Were the 'Fearless Iranians from Hell', those hardcore American punks, our only claim to rock and roll fame?

Although certainly overshadowed by the cultures of India and Morocco, that of Iran was by no means absent from the rock and roll repertoire of the twentieth century. As a result of a longstanding colonial history, India to the British wasn't exactly *terra incognita*. As well, Morocco in the fifties had become the haunt of Beat poets such as Kerouac, Ginsberg, and Burroughs[3], whose writings were followed closely by Americans and Brits alike. India was synonymous with spirituality, freedom, and man's search for meaning, while Tangier (and what had ere been the International Zone) with sex, drugs, and the 'otherworldliness' of North Africa. Considering this, it doesn't come as a surprise that super-groups such as the Beatles and the Stones chose to find inspiration there (amongst other things). Was Iran, under the rule of the suave Western-friendly Shah, a mere afterthought? What had happened to the European fascination for all things Persian? There was once a time when Voltaire adored Sa'di (his moniker, in fact) and Zarathustra, Goethe bonded with Hafez, Paul Poiret threw sumptuous 'Persian Fêtes', Persian-themed vaudeville songs were in vogue, and the likes of Kandinsky, Matisse, and Picasso were inspired by languid Persian belles; but it seemed that the poets, philosophers, and benign world-conquerors of Iran's past had become, at least to the scruffy-haired rock and rollers of the sixties and seventies, the stuff of stodgy old schoolbooks and Orientalists (in the original non-Saidian sense of the term). Persian lambskin coats and Meher Baba's muted teachings may have been all the rage, but nonetheless, places like India and Morocco – owing to their aforementioned associations – seemed much more promising and colourful where rock and roll fantasies were concerned.

Performance, Nicolas Roeg and Donald Cammell's surreal 1968 film (released in 1970) starring Mick Jagger, Anita Pallenberg, and James Fox, is only one instance of Iran's role on the stage of twentieth-century rock and roll. In the same year, Paul McCartney visited Tehran with his then-girlfriend, Jane Asher[4]. Paul wasn't completely green with regard to Iran, though; while the Beatles were in the Bahamas filming *Help!* in 1965, they had met Soraya Esfandiary Bakhtiari, the former Queen of Iran[5]. This time, however, Paul and Jane – arriving from their spiritually enlightened sojourn in Rishikesh with the Maharishi Mahesh Yogi – stopped over briefly in the Iranian capital, where they enjoyed Persian food and the bubbly sounds of the *ghalyan*, and hung out with Iran's velvety-smooth 'King of Pop', Vigen Derderian. Having been described as flippant, and with a Persian vocabulary not extending beyond the words *aks nagir* ('don't take pictures'), some thought Paul was taking the piss[6]. For better or worse, no *tars* or *setars* made it into any future Beatles or Wings recordings; the Iranian 'chapter' was over – that bird had flown. But the Beatles *had* had an Iranian episode, at least.

Iranian culture had a much greater role to play in the history of twentieth-century rock and roll, though, its influence and associations extending far beyond Jagger and McCartney. In 1926, audiences in Milan were treated to Giacomo Puccini's *Turandot,* an opera based on Carlo Gozzi's eponymous 1762 play[7]. Taking its name from 'Turandokht' (lit. 'Daughter of Turan' in Persian)[8], Gozzi's play had its roots in a story from the *Haft Paykar (Seven Beauties)*, a poetic parable written by the twelfth-century Persian poet Nezami Ganjavi[9]. Incidentally, nearly fifty years after *Turandot's* Milan debut, Nezami again served as a musical muse and inspiration, in perhaps the least likely of contexts. Perhaps the Beatles' Iranian chapter really hadn't been closed once and for all. In the early seventies, a young Eric Clapton – adored by his guitar-slinging votaries as 'God' – found himself hopelessly in love with Pattie Boyd, George Harrison's then-wife[10]. Though Blind Faith had come to an end, he was in the presence of the Lord yet; during the conversion of a friend (Ian Dallas) to Islam, the virtuoso guitarist was given a copy of Nezami's *Layla and Majnun*[11], a story that would mark a defining moment in both Clapton's career as well as rock and roll history. Though Nezami's romance in his *Khamseh* (*Quintet*) is based on a pre-Islamic Arabic story dating from the seventh century[12], it is his Persian rendition in particular, that, amongst all others (e.g. that of Fuzuli), has received the lion's share of praise and recognition the world over[13]. Seeing a connection between the tragic tale of Qais (a.k.a. *Majnun*, the 'madman') and Layla – employed as a Sufi allegory by Nezami[14] – and his obsession with Boyd, Clapton penned *Layla*, the title track of *Layla and Other Assorted Love Songs*, his 1970 album recorded with the nascent Derek and the Dominos. Echoing the urgency and passion of Nezami's ecstatic verses, *Layla* added another page to the legacy of the medieval Persian master, albeit this time in the annals of rock and roll history. *Please don't say we'll never find a way*, adjured Clapton, *and tell me all my love's in vain*. A tip of the hat to Nezami from God himself? Far out.

* * *

Why do I only remember the summertime? On an August's day, which now seems like it was aeons ago, I wandered into a record store called 'Sonic Temple', or something along those lines. Baking in the backseat of my car was a paperback copy of Rumi's *Masnavi*, and burning a hole through my pants, a crumpled twenty-dollar bill. Being into the guitar and all, I'd heard about some bloke called Richard Thompson, who could work magic on his Stratocaster. I don't know why I bought the particular album I did; it just felt right. On the cover was a blue-eyed youth with rough, sinewy braids and a bright white turban, looking out, full of wonder and wanting, into the distance. I thought it was only a matter of aesthetics, like the out-of-this-world cover of *Their Satanic Majesties' Request*; Thompson looked as much of a Sufi in my eyes as Jagger did the Prince of Darkness. When I popped in the disc in my stereo, and those words poured down like silver, it all began to make sense: the separation of the lover and the Beloved, the wine of union, the divine ecstasy of it all: *Dancing till my feet don't touch the ground,* he sang on *Night Comes In*, to the sound of a throaty out-of-phase Strat and sparkly Persian *santur*; *I lose my mind and dance forever … turn my world around.* I couldn't help but recall the verses of the baking *Masnavi* and the visage of Rumi himself. I thought it was farfetched, but a bit of reading proved otherwise. Apparently, Richard and his then-wife, Linda, had converted to Islam in 1974, and went on to live in Sufi communes between 1975 and 1978[15]. While the couple's teacher had encouraged Linda's singing, he suggested Richard give up the electric guitar

once and for all. 'Look, my mullah doesn't want
me to play the electric guitar', Richard told his
manager, Jo Lustig, at the time[16]. Of course, the
fair-haired rock and roller did anything but, instead
taking cues from Rumi, the Persian mystic from
Balkh who gave to the world his whirling dervishes
and their musical ceremonies[17]. Richard's 'mullah'
may have frowned up on his disciple's ultimate
decision, but Rumi would have no doubt approved;
for, as he always believed, *There are a hundred ways to
kneel and kiss the ground[18]*.

If the Persian Sufi poets Nezami and Rumi had left
their mark on those two English guitar gods, it was
a much different poet who would come to forever
be associated with a group of San Franciscan
hippies. In *Performance*, a dolled-up Jagger related
the tale of Hassan Sabbah, the Isma'ili leader of
the notorious Assassins of Alamut, who, until their
defeat at the hands of Hulagu Khan and the
Mongols, struck terror into all those who happened
to incur their dismay[19]. Although Sangorski and
Sutcliffe's jewel-encrusted copy of the *Robaiyat* –
'The Great Omar' – had long ago sunk to the sea
floor along with the Titanic[20], Edmund Joseph
Sullivan's illustrations for a 1913 edition of
Edward FitzGerald's interpretation of Omar
Khayyam's verses were still ripe for the picking.
Apparently, illustrators Stanley George Miller and
Alton Kelley (a.k.a. 'Mouse and Kelley') could
think of no finer illustration with which to adorn
the poster for the Grateful Dead's Avalon Ballroom

concerts in 1966 than one from Sullivan and FitzGerald's volume, in which a laughing skeleton stood surrounded by roses[21]. 'Kelley and I just looked at each other and said, "There it is – the perfect picture"', recalled Miller[22]. It was then that the 'skulls and roses' imagery surrounding the Dead first blossomed, and, so fitting was it that it later served as the cover artwork for the group's 1971 untitled album, affectionately known as *Skull Fuck*[23].

Although that particular illustration wasn't chosen solely on account of its aesthetics, Mouse and Kelley may not have been aware of the parallels between their philosophy and that of the eleventh-century Persian polymath. 'The skeleton symbolised death, and the roses symbolised rebirth and love', said Miller[24]. Death, rebirth, and love – are these three themes not central to the spirit of the *Robaiyat* that FitzGerald strove to capture in his own words?

> *As the New Year's spring clouds wash the tulip's visage,*
> *Arise, and fill the wine goblets with firm resolve.*
> *For this grass on which you recline today*
> *Shall sprout tomorrow from your ashes tall.*[25]

Whether they knew it or not, Mouse and Kelley's reasons for choosing the now-famous illustration had everything to do with Khayyam's own *Weltanschauung.* Talk about a 'skull fuck'.

Incidentally, five years after the release of *Skull Fuck*, another psychedelic West Coast American group with roots in the music of the Dead would establish a Persian connection. Only active between 1975 and 1976[26], the Relatively Clean Rivers released a self-titled album in the latter year, seemingly inspired by Biblical motifs. The songs *Babylon*, *Flight to Eden*, and *The Persian Caravan* all evoke images of passages in Abrahamic scripture dealing with Iran, particularly Cyrus the Great's conquest of Babylon in the mid-sixth century BC and his subsequent liberation of its oppressed Jews[27]; and, in listening to such tracks as *The Persian Caravan*, vinyl addicts might be hard-pressed to not make a connection to the oeuvre of The Orient Express, a trio from New York City's East Village involving one Farshid Golesorkhi, a percussionist who had gone so far as to receive the attention of the Shah of Iran[28]. Now obscure like the Rivers, The Orient Express' 1969 album saw the intersection of Western instrumentation and Eastern (particularly Indo-Iranian and Arabic) sensibilities. There were no references or nods to poets and mystics as in the case of Thompson and the Dead, but rather, raucous freak-outs and mash-ups in the vein of John Berberian and Ananda Shankar, of which *Azaar* [sic.] (Persian for 'fire'), with its lethargic Persian polyphony, is a shining example.

The aforesaid Persian connections, such as Thompson's electric, Rumi-inspired wanderings and Clapton's kinship with the crazed Qais are perhaps reflective of those on a substantive, quasi-spiritual plane. The role of Iran and Persian culture on the rock and roll stage of the twentieth century was not always one of depth; but then again, a bit of good old gobbledegook never hurt anyone. Marc Bolan, the diminutive wild child of Britain's seventies glam scene, had already flirted with Eastern imagery in his early years with Tyrannosaurus Rex before he made it big. *Afghan Woman* and *Evenings of Damask*, although boasting titular references to exoticised Eastern lands (the former Iranic), had little, if anything at all, to do with them. Likewise, his self-description as a 'labourer of love' in 'Persian gloves' in T. Rex's 1971's hit single *Hot Love*, can be taken equally as seriously, and be attributed more to simple wordplay than anything else in a song comprised mostly of cloying *la la la*s.

On the same side of the pond, shortly after Iranian youth had fought in the streets, set Tehran ablaze, and protested in the Big Apple with Patti Smith, the German instrumentalist Holger Czukay (of Krautrock band extraordinaire Can) found himself picking up strange voices on the radio in his Cologne laboratory. As the Scottish novelist Alan Warner recounted in a 2002 essay, Czukay had chanced upon a pair of Persian voices – one male, one female – on a Radio Tehran programme while fiddling around with his radio[29]. Enticed by their 'soaring minaret vocalisations', they ultimately found their way onto a 1979 single, fittingly titled *Persian Love*, with *Cool in the Pool* on the B-side. As with *Hot Love* and the Eastern-inspired songs of the twentieth-century boy, rhyme and reason seem to have little room in Czukay's electronic gambolling; could this be intentional? After all, in the Persian Sufi tradition, *Reason is powerless in the expression of love* – or so Rumi once said. Indeed, it was an expression of love, more than anything else, that had captivated Czukay, and listeners such as rock and roll bassist Jah Wobble. 'The voices on it are so beautiful,' Wobble is noted to have said upon listening to *Persian Love*, 'I will never, never try to sing again!'[30] With its melange of twittering synthesisers, crackly Radio Tehran vocals, and loose form, it strikes the ear as the perfect score to a scene from Khayyam's *Robaiyat*, replete with cypress trees, bare-chested beauties, and jugs brimming with blood-red wine: exactly the sort of image depicted on the single's cover, ostentatiously mimicking the Persian miniatures of Safavid-era Iran. *Many a time did we weather the flames of sorrow*, says the sultry-sounding hostess of the *Gol-ha* (*Flowers*) programme to Akbar Golpayegani (a.k.a. 'Golpa'), *and then, in the flames of sorrow did we burn.* Doubtless would Reza Shah have stroked his imperial whiskers in approval at such expressions of love straddling Krautrock and the Persian *avaz* tradition.

* * *

At first glance (or listen, rather), the vast majority of twentieth-century rock and roll suggests that all roads lead to India and Morocco, where foreign influences are concerned. As evinced, however, a bit of digging here and there reveals the lost Persian treasures glimmering beneath orbs of vinyl and cardboard, between reels of cellulite. While it can be shown that Iran and Persian culture were indeed present in the collective consciousness of Western rock and rollers, one wonders whether there were others like Golesorkhi and the Iranian writer-cum-songstress Shusha Guppy (née Shamsi Assar), who were not only active in Western circles, but also of Iranian origin themselves. The Armenians had Cher, and, while not exactly rock and roll, Aznavour was, and is, around nonetheless. Dylan had a pinch of Turkish blood in him[31], and there was no doubting Zappa's part-Arab ancestry[32] (celebrated in his booty-shaking alter-ego, Sheik Yerbouti). Did Iranians have anyone to call their own? Who was bearing the torch and kindling the flame of *Puhshhia?* Well, there *was* one such chap, in fact.

I remember not caring too much for this particular kid in grade school, who had this album he always carried around with him. It was burgundy in colour, and embellished with a dulled golden insignia that looked as if it had been taken from a banknote or passport. On the back was a picture of what seemed like a bunch of poster boys for bad British teeth and perms gone horribly, horribly wrong. I didn't find anything attractive about either them or the music (I was only eleven, for Christ's sake), although my mother begged to differ. 'Your friend has good taste', she told me, when *We are the Champions* came on the car radio one evening, and I mentioned the kid in question. She went on to describe the moustachioed man I'd seen on the back of the burgundy album to unbelieving ears; I was incredulous. 'What do you mean, "He's Iranian"? He's popular, Mum; people *love* him. They *know* him. How can an *Iranian* be cool?' It sounded like a tall tale: my second cousin had apparently given my grandmother the scoop, who'd told my aunt in turn, who'd told my father, who'd told my mother. I had played broken telephone at school, and, knowing all too well the explosive Iranian cocktail that is one part exaggeration and another hearsay, had my doubts. Come on – Freddie's real name is … *Farrokh?*

Grandma & co. may have been wrong about his last name being 'Jiveh' ('mercury' in Persian), but were bang on the money otherwise. A few months ago, when penning my novella, *Coming Down Again,* I found myself, in the torn sneakers of my protagonist, dreaming of becoming the world's first Iranian rock and roll star. *But wait a minute*, I thought to myself, *there's already been one*. If there will be another one, he or she will simply be carrying the banner of the greatest there's ever been: Freddie Mercury. Freddie, or, *Farrokh,* may not have been born in Iran, but he was Iranian to the bone.

A Parsi (meaning, literally, 'Persian'), his ancestors – Iranian Zoroastrians[33] – had left Iran for India in waves of migrations (beginning in the eighth century[34]), following the seventh-century Muslim conquest of their homeland[35]. Though more of a good old-fashioned lover boy than a Parsi one, his parents were steadfast Zoroastrians, the likes of which never married outside their community, and who prided themselves on their ancient Iranian heritage. Though this fact has been mentioned time and time again, it is yet little-known amongst his scores of followers, and, when divulged, often met with resistance. Is the world not ready for an Iranian rock and roll star, and a Zoroastrian one to boot? Owing to Farrokh having been Persian, Queen's records were given the green light in Iran in the early 'naughties'[36] – no small thing, considering that rock and roll and pop music as they were then known, were, for all practical purposes, outlawed there. Moreover, as with his sexuality, he was open when it came to his roots, and was never one to play things down. Keith Richards once said that if one is going to kick authority in the teeth, they might as well use both feet. So, was Farrokh Bulsara … *Persian?* He put it somewhat less subtly: '*I'll always walk around like a Persian popinjay, and no one's gonna stop me, honey!*'[37]

* * *

Following the Revolution, the tune – with the exception of anomalies such as Czukay's *Persian*

Love – largely changed. Ayatollah Khomeini had come and gone, and Freddie's spirit would soon spread its wings and fly away. In lieu of dancing dervishes and star-crossed sweethearts, the Clash were rocking the *casbah*, and Fearless Iranians from Hell dying for Allah, burning books, and blowing up the embassy. The 'Sharif ' who didn't like 'it' was none other than Khomeini, who had gotten on Joe Strummer's bad side on account of his banning rock and roll in Iran[38]. There weren't any overt references, however, to either Iran or Khomeini in 1982's *Rock the Casbah*, and the Turkish-born[39] Strummer's lyrics – which would later be revived by a man from the *casbah*s of Algeria, Rachid Taha – read more like jumbled-up Orientalist drivel than anything else (electric camel drums? *Muezzins* on radiator grilles?). *By order of the prophet*, growled a bellicose Strummer, black Telecaster in hand, *we ban that boogie sound!*

If the Clash's Persian Gulf War anthem[40] had alluded to Khomeini and the Revolution, the references made by another group of English punks years earlier had been anything but indirect. In their 1979 song *Shah Shah a Go Go*, The Stranglers chronicled, in biting, choppy verses doused in synthesisers and one-fingered riffery the downfall of the Pahlavi dynasty and Khomeini's rise to power. Sinister and industrial in tone, and with an ambience of impending doom, the flippant track seemed to echo the howl of the 'machine' Jalal Al-e Ahmad had so feared[41]. For a product of caustic English punk rock, *Shah Shah a Go Go* not only provided a soundtrack for errant youth, but also a history lesson. After setting the atmosphere with a foreboding call to prayer (sung by a *muezzin* on a radiator grille, perhaps?), a fervid Hugh Cornwell, to the backbeat of a drum machine, gave a crash course on the Iranian Revolution: his kind just had to *fa-fa-fade*, the man who used to live out in Iran and was 'luxury's greatest fan'. Cornwell's Shah had sold the English all their oil and made his people work the soil, until there came a 'priest from Paris, France' (i.e. Khomeini, who spent the last years of his exile not in Paris, but Neauphle-le-Château[42]), who distributed cassettes that made his followers *da-da-dance*. Would Khomeini set the people free, as Cornwell had remembered him promise? The doom and gloom he painted – reflected in the single's austere cover – along with his sarcasm suggested otherwise: *We shall see, we shall see …*

Similarly, the Spanish director Pedro Almodóvar also toyed around with the subject of the Iranian Revolution, on both a cinematic and musical plane. Far from creating a soundscape of grandeur and mystery, such as that of *Persepolis*, a track by the Spanish group Los Pekenikes, released in 1971 (the same year as the Shah's bombastic celebrations of the twenty-five hundredth anniversary of the founding of the Persian Empire in Persepolis), the auteur instead lampooned the deposed Pahlavi dynasty with his trademark blend of kitsch and flamboyant sexuality. In *Labyrinth of Passion* (1982), Riza Niro, the son of the Emperor of 'Tiran' and the barren Princess 'Toraya' (it isn't particularly difficult to make the connections to Crown Prince Reza Pahlavi, the Shah, and Queen Soraya Esfandiary Bakhtiari), disguises himself as Johnny, a punk, in order to evade Sadec, a member of a terrorist organisation (a far cry from Voltaire's Zoroastrian hero, Zadig) looking for Riza. In one of the film's highlights, Riza fills in for Eusebio – the lead singer of the band 'Ellos' – to sing *Gran Ganga* (*The Great Bargain*), a song written by Almodóvar himself during his days in the punk act Almodóvar and McNamara[43]. *Sex, luxury, and paranoia – that's been my fate*, sings Riza, before diving into the tune's boisterously camp chorus: *Gran ganga, gran ganga – I am from Tehran!*

* * *

What, after the Revolution, happened to Jagger's stories about the Old Man of the Mountain and his damsel-strewn paradise, to Bolan's velveteen Persian gloves, to the love stories of Nezami Ganjavi that had tugged at the strings of Clapton's heart and guitar alike? They were ravaged, perhaps, not by the flames of love, but the vicissitudes of cruel time. Iran still served as a creative stimulus, albeit in a much different way. Mockery, belittlement, and vilification became the norm, concomitant with a transformation of Iran, in popular Western culture, from exotic, innocuous realm (although, as many noted, under the rule of a despot) to flag-burning *bête noire*. Iran and twentieth-century Western rock and roll may today seem to be stark opposites of each other, as they did to me as a child. They may appear to the neophyte as irreconcilable, as two spirits diametrically opposed to one another in a sort of Manichean polarisation. 'East is East,' once wrote Kipling, 'and West is West, and never the twain shall meet'. But they did; and 'meet' is an understatement at best. Once, not too long ago, did groupies dream of becoming bandits in the mountains of Persia, guitar slingers drink the 'wine of lovers' and dance in the footsteps of Rumi, till their feet could no longer feel the ground beneath them, and a toothy Persian popinjay conquer the world, with a crown atop his head.

And it was beautiful.

5/10/2016

Bibliography

1. Performance [film]. Directed by Nicolas Roeg and Donald Cammell. UK: Warner Bros., 1970.
2. Bream, J., Honey, P., ed. *Whole Lotta Led Zeppelin.* London: Voyageur Press, 2010.
3. Jordison, S. *Beat and Dust: Tangier's Tang of History* [online]. 2010. [Accessed 27 April 2016]. Available from: http://www.theguardian. com/

books/booksblog/2010/nov/23/tangier-william- burroughs-naked-lunch.

4. Mehdizadeh, M. *Beatelha: Rock's Early Days in Iran* [online]. 1996. [Accessed 27 April 2016]. Available from: http://iranian.com/ Jan96/ Articles/Beatelha.html.

5. Kadivar, D. *Help! Princess Soraya Greeted by the Beatles in the Bahamas* [online]. 2011. [Accessed 27 April 2016]. Available from: http:// iranian.com/main/blog/darius-kadivar/help-princess-soraya-greeted-beatles- bahamas.html.

6. Mehdizadeh, M. *Beatelha: Rock's Early Days in Iran* [online]. 1996. [Accessed 27 April 2016]. Available from: http://iranian.com/ Jan96/ Articles/Beatelha.html.

7. The Metropolitan Opera. *Puccini: Turandot* [online]. 2015. [Accessed 27 April 2016]. Available from: http://www.metopera. org/ metoperafiles/education/Educator%20Guides/ Ed%20Gu ide%20pdfs/Turandot.guide.pdf.

8. Young, J.B. *Puccini: A Listener's Guide.* Mineola: Dover, 2016.

9. Packhard Humanities Institute – Persian Literature in Translation. *"Niz̄āmī" Ganjavī, Jamāl al-Dīn Abū Muh̄ammad Ilyās* [online]. [Accessed 27 April 2016]. Available from: http://persian.packhum. org/persian/bio? anum=0176.

10. *Pattie Boyd – The Story Behind Eric Clapton's 'Layla'.* The Ronnie Wood Show (Sky Arts), August 2013.

11. Boyd, P. *Wonderful Tonight – George Harrison, Eric Clapton, and Me*. New York City: Three Rivers Press, 2007.
12. Seyed-Gohrab, A.A. *Leili o Majnun* [online]. 2009. [Accessed 27 April 2016]. Available from: http://www.iranicaonline.org/articles/leyli-o-majnun-narrative- poem.
13. Bodleian Libraries. *Layla and Majnun* [online]. [Accessed 27 April 2016]. Available from: http://www.bodleian.ox.ac.uk/whatson/discover/online/love-and- devotion/layla-and-majnun.
14. Henderson, B. *Radical Muslim Leader Has Past in Swinging London* [online]. 2010. [Accessed 27 April 2016]. Available from: http://www.telegraph.co.uk/news/worldnews/7271752/Radical-Muslim-leader- has-past-in-swinging-London.html.
15. Young, R. *Electric Eden: Unearthing Britain's Visionary Music*. London: Faber and Faber, 2010.
16. Humphries, P. *Richard Thompson – The Biography*. New York City: Schirmer Trade Books, 1997.
17. Hoyestad, O.M. *A History of the Heart*. London: Reaktion Books, 2009.
18. Rumi, Barks, C., trans. *The Book of Love – Poems of Ecstasy and Longing*. San Francisco: HarperCollins, 2013.
19. Hourcade, B. *Alamut* [online]. 15 December 1985. [Accessed 28 April 2016]. Available from: http://www.iranicaonline.org/ articles/alamut-valley-alborz- northeast-of-qazvin-.

·

20. Massey, L. *Jewels & Illuminations: Sangorski & Sutcliffe* [online]. 2012. [Accessed 28 April 2016]. Available from: http://www.peterharrington.co.uk/blog/jewels-illuminations-sangorski-sutcliffe/.

21. Grimes, W. *Alton Kelley, 67, Artist of the 1960s Rock Counterculture, Dies* [online]. 2008. [Accessed 28 April 2016]. Available from: http://www.nytimes.com/2008/06/04/arts/design/04kelley.html?_r=0.

22. Dark Star Palace. *'Skull Fuck' Cover Art and the Rubaiyat* [online]. 2010. [Accessed 28 April 2016]. Available from: http://www.darkstarpalace.com/2010_06_01_archive.html.

23. Ibid.

24. Ibid.

25. Bekhrad, J. *The Quatrains of Omar Khayyam*. Bloomington: Balboa Press, 2017.

26. Rising Storm. *Relatively Clean Rivers (Review)* [online]. 2007. [Accessed 28 April 2016]. Available from: http://therisingstorm. net/relatively-clean-rivers-self- titled/.

27. Dandamayev, M.A. *Cyrus* [online]. 1993. [Accessed 28 April 2016]. Available from: http://www.iranicaonline.org/articles/cyrus-iii.

28. The Orient Express (liner notes). Mainstream Records, 1969.

29. Warner, A. Persian Love. *Granta*, 2001, 1(76).

30. Ibid.

31. Ebiri, B. *We are All Bob Dylan: Turkish Dylan* [online]. 5 October 2007. [Accessed 28 April 2016]. Available from: http://www.

vulture.com/2007/10/
we_are_all_bob_dylan_turkish_d.html#.

32. Arab American Institute. *Famous Arab Americans* [online]. [Accessed 28 April 2016]. Available from: http://www.aaiusa.org/ famous-arab-americans.

33. Bhatia, S. *Freddie Mercury's Family Tell of Singer's Pride in His Asian Heritage* [online]. 2011. [Accessed 28 April 2016]. Available from: http://www.telegraph.co.uk/culture/music/music-news/8828994/ Freddie- Mercurys-family-tell-of-singers-pride-in-his-Asian-heritage.html.

34. Hinnels, John R. and Alan Williams, eds. *Parsis in India and the Diaspora*. New York: Routledge, 2007.

35. Guzer, D. *The Last of the Zoroastrians* [online]. 2008. [Accessed 29 April 2016]. Available from: http://content.time.com/time/world/article/ 0,8599,1864931,00.html.

36. BBC News. *Queen Album Brings Rock to Iran* [online]. 2004. [Accessed 29 April 2016]. Available from: http://news.bbc.co.uk/2/ hi/ entertainment/3593532.stm.

37. Queen. *Freddie Mercury – The Official Birthday Video* [online]. 2011. [Accessed 29 April 2016]. Available from: https://www.youtube.com/ watch?v=Uuqx11UOOP4.

38. Marcus, G. The Last Broadcast. In: D'Ambrosio, A., ed. *Let Fury Have the Hour: Joe Strummer, Punk, and the Movement that Shook the*

World. New York City: Nation Books, 2012, pp. 61 – 73.

39. Rolling Stone. *Joe Strummer – Biography* [online]. [Accessed 29 April 2016]. Available from: http://www.rollingstone.com/music/ artists/ joe- strummer/biography.

40. Farzanefar, A. *Anthem of US Marines: 25 Years of Rock the Casbah* [online]. [Accessed 30 April 2016]. Available from: https:// en.qantara.de/ content/25-years- of-rock-the-casbah-anthem-of-us-marines.

41. Al-i Ahmad, J., Campbell, R., trans. *Occidentosis: a Plague from the West.* Berkeley: Mizan Press, 1984.

42. Moin, B. *Khomeini: Life of the Ayatollah.* London: I.B. Tauris, 1999.

43. Thornburgh, N. *The Gift of Wild Possibility* [online]. [Accessed 30 April 2016]. Available from: http://www.thestranger.com/seattle/ the-gift-of-wild- possibility/Content?oid=9500.

Across the Universe

Musings on 'Home Ground: Contemporary Art from the Barjeel Art Foundation' at the Aga Khan Museum

'No, I'm not him', I say with a smile, returning my gaze to the photograph before me while brushing a hand through a thicket of coarse curls. Though I've let them down, their giggles and hushed chatter linger on. I've been mistaken for Tahar Rahim – known to the twenty-something girls as 'the guy in the video'[1] – who, moments earlier, was passionately pressing his lips against those of Fanny Ardant in a picturesque desert landscape, before resigning himself to a fate of exile and the unknown. Sipping quietly on a soon-to-be-gone glass of chardonnay, I find myself transfixed by a rather unassuming piece that has been largely overlooked by the silk-draped, stilettoed throng. A block of ice, consummately sculpted by the Lebanese artist Joseph Charbel H. Boutros (for whom I've also been mistaken), is lying modestly amidst foliage by a riverbank[2]. The composition, though almost deceptively simple and facile, belies a haunting quality and poetic beauty. Essaying to depict the struggle involved in leaving one's home and later returning to it, Boutros moulded the block of ice from the river, and later submerged the

---

* A reference to Youssef Nabil's *You Never Left* (2010)

[2] A reference to Joseph Charbel Boutros' *From Water to Water* (2013)

mass within it again. Though the matter completes a 'cycle', it is not an effortless one; it has been removed from its natural environment, and, in becoming frozen, has had its state altered. To return to its origin, it will need to melt and dissolve back into the river, assuming shapes and forms far less romantic than Boutros' sugar cube-like figure. It may complete the cycle once; or, it may be forced to undertake it again, depending on its fortune. In either case, neither shall the mass of water remain the same, nor the depths from which it arose.

Like Boutros' block, I have repeatedly undergone such transformative cycles – or so I think. I left Iran with my parents at the age of one, and began making regular visits there many years later as a teenager. I still think of Iran as home, though soon after the excitement of landing in Tehran dissipates and the smell of petrol and burning wild rue become all too familiar, I'm reminded that I'm light years away from any notion of 'home'. Having lived the greater part of my life – and the formative one, at that – between North America and western Europe, I'm a far different person than the Joobin who might have stayed behind in Iran in the eighties and become a *Tehrani* through and through. Though I often don't like to admit it, I'm very much a stranger in a strange land, a condition I think will little change as time goes on. I may submerge myself in my beloved homeland from time to time for weeks – and months – on end, but, come what may, I'll always dream in English, think in English, and let out the odd accidental *'yeah'* and *'umm'* here and there. I have, however, developed a peculiar tendency (and proficiency) to curse in Persian rather tastefully – a fact by which yours truly is deservingly chuffed.

If, while looking at Boutros' harrowing black-and-white photograph, but one consoling thought permeates the unruly brambles strewn over my ears and brow – other than the fact that I smell 'exceedingly of flowers', as one onlooker has told me – it is that I am not alone. An hour earlier, as we sipped on wine and sweated through our every orifice, Suheyla and I chatted about the experience and oft-accepted state of nomadism in the twenty-first century. Upon hearing the word 'nomad', Tasleem – another of the 'tribe' – joined us from afar. So much for being the displaced dreamer of the night, I thought to myself, albeit not with surprise; after all, the entire premise of the evening was an exploration of what Suheyla referred to in languid tones that fell on my ears like birdsong amidst the babble as 'Sisyphean' struggles. 'Do you know Sisyphus?' she asked, as if he were present amongst the motley crowd. I found it hard to respond in a way that wasn't gauche: 'Uh, yeah', I said, after thinking for a moment that she'd enquired about an STD. *Sisyphus* … the name reverberated in my head, while a few footsteps away, Sultan whizzed about like a butterfly on speed, a childlike twinkle in his eye all the while.

Joobin Bekhrad

* * *

Cactus, we meet again. I had first seen Asim Abu Shakra's solemn painting of a potted cactus on a windowsill[3] at Sultan Sooud Al Qassemi's Dubai dwelling a few months back, just before the sun-worshippers ate their words. I'd had one too many bottomless glasses of choice merlot, and, distracted by the flowing tresses of one whose name now escapes me, was finding it rather trying to listen to Sultan as he hurriedly told us the story behind the not-just-any-old-cactus. A leitmotif in Shakra's work, the cactus has served both as a symbol in Israeli and Palestinian narratives. To Shakra – as with his compatriots – it stood as a metaphor for the Palestinian struggle: a cactus plant can survive in the harshest of conditions; sprouting from its native soil, it stands its ground aright and proud as an often solitary figure in a barren landscape. Left alone, it is unimposing and keeps to itself; provoke it, however, and it is quick to prick. Though in Tel Aviv, Shakra forgot not his motherland and the *résistance*. Perhaps a memento from his native Umm el Fahm, it found its way to the 'other side' in Tel Aviv, and, from there, journeyed across borders and boundaries to the Emirates, God knows where else, and now, Toronto, of all places. I find it rather heartwarming that my drunken meeting with the prickly *déraciné* was not to be my last, and that we – two drifters 'off to see the world', to quote Ol' Blue

---

[3] A reference to Asim Abu Shakra's *Cactus* (1989)

Eyes – have found each other again in 'Terannah', as Sultan likes to call it.

How I evny Handala; Handala, barefoot with his back to my face, his hands crossed in resignation, looking almost as if pinioned[†]. Won't you give us a smile, Handala? *Ah, but you have no mouth.* Won't you look upon this lonely one, *ya* Handala? *Ah, but you have no eyes.* Handala, you see, has long been waiting, and will long wait yet. It is said that he will only deign to turn around and break his silence once those from yonder leave his land, and let his people go. 'His land' – can the same term be used in reference to me? At the very least, this oblong caricature knows whom and what he's fighting for, and, like my friend the cactus, stands his ground with pride and purpose. I know well that I'm a dreamer, that I see my beloved through rose-tinted glasses, beyond the sage boughs and creepers of a rambling mind. Does what I dream of exist, or, am I just a helpless, starry-eyed romantic? *Wipe clean the pages if a confidante art thou, for cannot love's ways in a book be found.*

* * *

'This is Joobin – he's from Canada', said Sultan earlier, introducing me to a friend. I was left dumbfounded.

'Err … I'm Iranian, although … I suppose –'

Joobin Bekhrad

'– So you're Canadian, then?'

Yes, I'm Canadian; *but why does this have to be so hard?*
Would that I could introduce myself as an old soul
from the forests of Hyrcania, from a magical realm
which may or may not exist …

* * *

Splashes of suitcases, jocund yet unsettling[4], come
to occupy the corner of my eye. Mementos of a
bloody civil war though they be, they're jarringly
familiar to me. Just as the constant thought of
having to flee and relocate weighed heavily upon
Baalbaki in wartime Beirut, so does it on my mind.
I sometimes think it's to do with the way I've been
wired, that it's simply in my blood as an Iranian.
How often would I daydream as a bored university
student about the migrations of the ancient Indo-
Iranians, those noble fleet-footed horsemen
commanding swift chariots through the harsh and
unforgiving steppes before descending into the
Iranian plateau, the subcontinent, and elsewhere.
The names of tribes peppered throughout the
books of Herodotus and Xenophon fascinated me:
Scythians, Sarmatians, Alans; though of many
only names and vestiges remain, their spirits loom
large within me. Not considering any physical
place to be 'home', I have little attachments to my
surroundings, and often feel the need to simply …

---

[4] A reference to Mohamad Said Baalbaki's *Heap* (2014)

move. Even when comfortably settled in some sleepy town or other, I instinctively think about how I will take my belongings with me around the world – usually consisting of skinny jeans, secondhand books, and electric guitars – should I decide to call it a day tomorrow. I've become accustomed to living out of suitcases, those damned vessels that have taken to chasing my silhouette like spectres. This feeling of homelessness, of the impulse to perpetually wander and wend, is something I've come to coin 'Sindbad Syndrome'. That intrepid, foolhardy sailor, however, eventually found his way home (not unlike Boutros' block of ice) after his seven daring voyages, until he was ultimately seized by the Destroyer of Delights. I, on the other hand, am still searching for it.

* * *

You are still here. Tell me, O Mona, I think to myself, *where do I go?* Her infinity symbol[5] reminds me of my alter-ego Tahar, who in ethereal hues and landscapes is forever leaving and returning, leaving and returning. 'I've got no place, no address', he says amongst the stars. We're not so different after all, you and I – although the giggling girls are long gone. Mona's words carry a sense of urgency, and I don't care to think of what 'you' and 'here' in this context mean to her; they mean something to *me*,

---

[5] References to Mona Hatoum's *Infinity* (2009) and *You Are Still Here* (2013)

and that's enough. Youssef tells me that with displacement comes the hope of rebirth and renewal, of renaissance. I have yet to experience such 'rebirths'. Toronto bores me, London kills me, Tehran breaks me to pieces, and everywhere else seems imaginary; yet, what else can I do but continue searching for somewhere bearing some semblance to what I've never known as 'home'? What else can Sisyphus do but continue to bear the brunt of his load upwards, ever onwards? We're damned if we do, and damned if we don't. At the same time, I find something romantic, almost otherworldly, in the pursuit for a place to call my own. For as long as I've known, I've been running along the sands of an endless shore; ah, the sweetness of the moment I shall utter those glorious words: 'The sea! The sea!'

Do you know Sisyphus? Suheyla's question rings again in my head, this time with added poignancy – perhaps as a result of the chardonnay. *Yeah, I know Sisyphus alright …*

8/4/2015

'Home Ground: Contemporary Art from the Barjeel Art Foundation' ran between July 25, 2015 and January 3, 2016 at the Aga Khan Museum in Toronto.

The Place to Which I Shall Return

> 'Home is not where you were born. Home is where all your attempts to escape cease.'
> – Naguib Mahfouz

I'm fiddling around with a cracked peanut shell in my hand, eyeing weary moustachioed faces and green-tinged cheeks. I don't speak Turkish, but can make out a few words here and there in between sips of what will probably be the last proper beer I'll have in what seems to me like a lifetime. My gaze falls on the fluorescent lights of the little stalls below the makeshift lounge. Feeling a bit heady, the sonorous song of a lovelorn Turk dripping from my ears, I marvel at the power of the bottle, the boutique, and the bar; had we these three, would we be so quick as to jump headlong into the first plane to take us to swanky 'Stamboul and Dubai down under? Maybe, maybe not. We might not have had democracy before the Revolution – the ominous 'R' word – but we had booze aplenty, and no need to throw around our hard-earned *tomans* in the land of the Grand Turk and the Arabian shores of the Persian Gulf.

I was never around to experience those heady halcyon days (or so they call them); all I have are the stories recounted to me by my parents and relatives. Forget about Istanbul and Dubai – even faraway places like the States and Britain held little appeal for many. Upon finishing his studies in the

US, my father had plans to settle down there with my mother, which my grandfather couldn't fathom. 'Sonny boy,' he said, 'what business do you have in America? Come back to Iran, the land of roses and nightingales.' My parents did eventually return to Iran in the seventies – in the winter of '78, at the zenith of the Revolution – but my father had had a bad feeling all along about the future of his country; even whilst in Portland, he knew things were changing. Being the staunch monarchists they were, however, my grandparents wouldn't hear any of it. 'The Shah leave Iran? *Impossible.* Bite your tongue, young man!' We had it all back then, as some will tell you; and, just a few years later, we lost it all. Everything.

I keep looking at my phone (I'm too hip for watches) to check the time, and my ticket to double and triple-check my flight details. In around half-an-hour or so, I'll be on my way across fabled Anatolia – the land of my beloved Yashar Kemal and the legendary bandit Koroğlu – and the windy Caucasus Mountains to what I have always regarded as 'home', yet which I know will never be. I can't say whether I'm happy, depressed, or anxious, as I feel all three emotions at once. Though I should, for all practical purposes, be ecstatic to be returning for a month, I can't help but feel an inexplicable heaviness in my heart; perhaps it's because whenever I travel to Iran, I feel like I'm visiting another world – which I am, in a sense. Iran isn't exactly like other countries; it's literally in a category of its own. When I go to Iran, I don't just kiss cold pints of lager goodbye, but also everything I'm used and accustomed to, and which I take for granted on a daily basis. Sure, we have the Internet, but it requires, as is often said, the patience of Ayoub; and besides, most of the sites I visit are blocked. Everyone there uses VPNs ('filter-breakers', as they like to call them), but even those don't work too well, and nothing is ever guaranteed. The speed is so slow that oftentimes checking emails becomes a Sisyphean task, and, accordingly, before going to Iran, I usually tell my colleagues and friends to not bother getting in touch whatsoever.

As with the Internet, you can find anything you want in Iran if you have the will and drive to do so; however, what you find usually has to be attained through illicit means (fancy a glass of Shiraz? You'll have to have that delivered to you in a brown paper bag by a seedy-looking man on a motorbike), over-payment (e.g. in the case of certain articles of branded clothes from abroad), or behind closed doors and curtains (orgies, anyone?). Not to worry, though; for everything you're acclimatised but don't have recourse to, there's a wholesome, family-friendly, good old-fashioned Iranian alternative. Instead of an ice-cold Heineken, for instance, you and your friends can have fun with a plastic two-litre bottle of 0.0% Delster to enjoy along with a bowl of pistachios nuts. And of course, it's largely the domestic products (*sakht-e Iran*) that are conspicuous throughout the city. Brands from the Far East also abound, but then again, where don't they? Cut off from all traces of the 'Global North' and the Western world I grew up in, and with a permit to stay for up to a maximum of three months and leave the country once a year (unless I'd like to serve in the military for two years), I often feel – after the excitement of my new surroundings fast dissipate – a sensation somewhere between suffocation, isolation, and unfamiliarity. Yes, my life – for the most part – revolves around Iran, but I personally like a bit of balance. At times, it simply gets a bit too much for me, and I feel the overwhelming urge to walk into a bar and hear the Stones on the radio; to flick on the television and see Bowie bandying around a guitar; to read a proper English book not belonging to the nineteenth century; and to gaze at eccentrics with blue hair on a vine-strewn cobblestone street in the stylish labyrinths of some urban European jungle. For all my nationalist sentiments and feelings of defiant pride, perhaps I'm more Western than I'd like to think. In Persian, there's a word for people like me, and it's not particularly pretty: *gharbzadeh*. I am one, who, in the philosophy of the late Jalal Al-e Ahmad, has been 'struck' by the epidemic of the West. *Khoda shafayam bedeh* – may God grant me health!

* * *

I rub my silver *farvahar* necklace as the plane hits the runway. The first time I landed in Tehran, I heard ejaculations of joy and claps; there aren't any this time, but I make nothing of it. I can feel damp patches underneath my arms, and the pungent smell of yesterday's cologne emanating from my chest. I wonder whether or not to button up my shirt and tuck in my pendants – the Zoroastrian *farvahar* and the Hindu *aum* – but later laugh at the idea, and think how much of an outsider I feel like. It was only last year that I was in Tehran to meet with local artists and visit my relatives, and I'm back again for the same reasons, more or less; I've also, of course, missed the place immensely. Standing in line at passport control, behind middle-aged ladies adjusting their headscarves and fanning themselves with their passports, I think about what to say if I'm questioned. It's an instinct, an impulse that comes on subconsciously; though I'm always quick to let people know I was born in Tehran, it's not a fact that comes in particularly helpful in transit. It doesn't matter that I've lived twenty-five out of the twenty-seven years I've been on this planet in Canada, and am a Canadian citizen; the mere mention of my birthplace is enough to spark suspicion and a flurry of questions at the airport, and, as such, I'm usually high-strung whilst waiting to have my passport examined. The finely chiselled fellow behind the Plexiglas window, looking like he's just emerged from a slab of Roman marble, beckons me with a glance to come forward. With a curt '*Salam*', I give him my passport from a sweaty hand, and, after a quick glance through its pages, his stamp comes pounding down. I'm on my way – no interrogations, no enquiries, no accusations. I've been to Tehran many times; yet, I always feel uneasy at the airport, on account of the largely rubbish stories my fellow compatriots – many of whom have almost zero ties to the country – tell one another during their regular gatherings. According to some of them, the majority of Iranians visiting the country from abroad are accused of being spies, hoarded on a bus, and taken straight to Evin Prison from the airport to waste away in squalor. 'Why would they do such a thing?' any sensible person would ask, to which the proverbial response would come: 'Ah, they don't need a reason – it's the Islamic Republic!' Truth be told, I've never had an easier time entering and leaving a country than in Iran, whereas I'm often in for unpleasant surprises back in Canada and Britain. The US is another story altogether.

The first familiar faces I see are not those of my grandparents, friends, or relatives, but rather of the late Ayatollah Khomeini and the current Supreme Leader, Ayatollah Khamenei. I've seen them so many times I feel I know them in a way, and their grey beards and turbans remind me of the pictures of my ancestors I often unearth from under my bed to peruse with elation. It's as if, in a grandfatherly sort of way, they're welcoming me back home, to my roots, to my *sarzamin*, to the land of the noble, bastion of the believers – Iran. They don't look particularly happy to see me, but I'm sure they are, deep down inside.

* * *

It's nearly three in the morning; a dishevelled heap of skin and bones, I don't bother shopping around for a cab driver, but rather jump into the first one I can find. I'm so focused on getting home and dropping dead after my journey halfway around the world – a 'journey to Kandahar', as per the saying – that I barely glance at the driver; I think he gets my drift, as he remains quiet during the entire trip – and it's not a short one, by any means. We're on the outskirts of the city, and have quite a way to go before we finally reach the beating, thumping heart of this metropolis that beguiles me, seduces me, enamours me, and disgusts me, all at once. I guess it's what one would call a love-hate relationship. I can't argue with that.

No sooner does the driver flick on the car stereo than we're on the highway towards the city. The song pouring forth from the speakers is characteristically Persian, sung in the classical vein. I'm not listening to the words, but rather looking outside at the bleak landscape. The singer is most probably reciting the heavenly verse of Hafez, Sa'di, or some other master, but, to my disinterested and weary ears, it sounds more funereal than mystical, a feeling that becomes accentuated as we pass by the massive Behesht-e Zahra cemetery. Somewhere amongst those myriad slabs of stone, I think to myself, lie the bones of my grandfather. I've never visited his grave, and probably never will; such structures have never held any importance for me, and I've never felt any need for them, either. I can feel my grandfather in my blood and bones, and don't need anyone, or thing, to remind me of the fact. Nonetheless, I try to imagine where his grave might be, saying a prayer in my heart all the while.

Whizzing past billboards in praise of Ali, microwaves, and biscuits, we drive past Ayatollah Khomeini's tomb and mosque, a grand golden edifice glimmering in the night sky, festooned with homely coloured bulbs in green, blue, and red. I try to close my eyes and catch up on some much-needed rest, but can't, for some reason, avert my gaze from the bleakness outside, which slowly begins to take on shape and form as we approach the belly of the beast. Hills emerge, as do high-rise buildings dotting the foothills of the Alborz Mountains where Arash the Archer once let loose his auspicious arrow. I can see, in the corner of my eye, the silver dome and minarets of a mosque, as well as the first of many martyr murals, strewn with tulips. Some of them look just like me. What would I have done had my parents decided to stay in Iran? Would I, who so proudly claim to be an Iranian and have Ferdowsi's ardent desire emblazoned upon my soul – *Should there be no Iran, may I cease to exist!* – have fought in the War? Would I, like those scores of countless children, have lunged forth at tanks with bare hands and walked over mines? I feel a cold chill run through my legs, and the hair on my arms stand on their ends. Why them, and not me?

The streets are unusually empty; had it been four in the afternoon rather than the morning, we would have been caught in a lethal deadlock, frying away beneath the beating sun. Everywhere I see neon signs, some flickering, some on, and some but outlines in the darkness. I lower the window, and a cool breeze smelling of gasoline and dust tosses my thick hair about in the wind. Behrouz Vossoughi and Naser Malekmotiee once strolled these streets looking for trouble, while Shahram Shabpareh drove about in his little jeep, probably en route to a gig at Koochini, Chatanooga, or one of the other popular haunts of yesteryear my father so often talks about excitedly. There's not a *chador*, *hejab*, or policeman in sight, and I lose myself in an early morning daydream as we breeze through boulevards, alleys, and Tehran's main drag, Vali-ye Asr Avenue. Her name may have changed throughout the cruel vicissitudes of time, but she'll always be beautiful to me, lined with her resplendent plane trees and running streams carrying manna from the mountains. Mossadegh, Pahlavi, Vali-ye Asr – they are names for one and the same, for Paradise.

At around five in the morning, we pull into a nondescript alley in Gheytarieh, a rather upper-class neighbourhood in the northeast. My grandparents having sold their apartment in Zafar last year, I don't have a place to stay anymore, and, as such, have rented an apartment for a month following the advice of a friend. Like the alley in which it's situated, the building is characterless, and anything but ostentatious. To no avail, I ring the superintendent to open the door. I feel like I'm two thousand light years from home, to quote the Stones, and, on top of that, am alone in the middle of Tehran in the wee hours of the morning with two suitcases in my hands.

Not a bad start to my sojourn, I think. Even the buzzer for the lower level is broken. In desperation, I give the owner of the building a rude awakening. A few minutes later, the door opens, and my eyes meet those of a smiling moustachioed man clad in baggy trousers and a grease-smeared tartan shirt. Clinging to him is a little girl with a ponytail, who looks at me warily from behind her father's legs. '*Agha* Mohammad?' I ask with trepidation. 'Yes, *agha* – welcome!' He's a cheery, good-natured fellow – especially for someone woken up at five in the morning – but that doesn't prevent me from heaping curses on him after he asks for my passport as 'security'. I still, of course, have my Canadian passport, but my Iranian one is my ticket out of this joint. Bloody hell – I have no passport, no home, and no idea as to what awaits me next.

Perhaps Rachid Taha put it best: *Andy wahloo! I have nothing baby – no-thing!*

* * *

I wince as I flick on the fluorescent lights in my bedroom. The place – sparsely furnished with only the barest of necessities – resembles more a prison than a flat. I'm famished, but all I have to snack on are cookies and sour cherry *sharbat*, the thought of which kills whatever appetite I might have had. I'm dirty, but have no towel to dry myself with, and bored, with only state television to watch. *That's alright*, I think to myself, *as long as there's a half-decent Internet connection, I'm a happy man*. I blow on my mobile for good luck, and invoke the name of the Prophet Zarathustra. '*Ya Zartosht!*' The circle – along with my head – is still spinning, and I'm sitting underneath the aura of the sickly fluorescent glow above me.

In futility, I curse greasy *Agha* Mohammad under my breath, streak my hands through my hair in exasperation, and hurl imprecations at the son-of-a-bitch secretary who got it into his mind to even consider this place for me; but I know it's just a stroke of bad luck, perhaps as a result of some black stray cat, or – more plausibly – my own stupidity at having left the business of finding a place until the last minute. There are apartment buildings, the likes of which I've never seen in Toronto or London, and glamorous neighbourhoods aplenty; all one needs to do is go for a spin (in perhaps the Maserati or Porsche of a parvenu) in the city's many upper-class districts such as Elahiyeh and Velenjak to have their jaw temporarily dislocated in awe. Gheytarieh, too, is looked kindly upon, and as such, I think it took a special talent to find this sorry excuse of a place. But, as they say, there's no use crying over spilt milk (or *doogh*, rather, in my case); I realise I'll be in the city for a month and had better get used to it, warts and all. If only I could see the mountains, though. If only.

* * *

I was born in the month of Aban – 'The Waters' – by the foothills of the Alborz Mountains, those stony ancient relics surrounding the city, on the same day as the once-Crown Prince of Iran, Reza Pahlavi. From over the hills and far away, explosive love letters from Saddam whizzed about in the air, occasionally landing in Tehran, as if to remind us that his war wasn't only being fought in the south and the wild west, but at our doorsteps as well. From the unassuming Asia Hospital, I was wrapped up in a blanket, popped in a basket, and taken back home; little did I know then what designs my parents had in mind for me. When it comes to the subject of post-Revolution immigrants and the Iranian diaspora, many assume that all families left primarily because of their unwillingness to live under the rule of the

Islamic Republic, and, in some cases, that they fled, being lucky to have 'escaped' in one piece. While such accounts very well exist, it certainly wasn't the case when it came to my family.

My parents met in Portland in the seventies, whilst studying at the university there. Despite having become accustomed to life in the land of milk and honey, they decided to move back to Iran in 1978, of all years, when revolutionary zeal was at its apex. In Tehran, amidst curfews, demonstrations, the commanding voice of Khomeini, and memories of the Shah, my parents enjoyed a makeshift wedding in the apartment of my grandparents' Jewish neighbours. It was anything but glamorous: relatives (the ones who could fit in the tiny place) brought gasoline as a present, my father had to dodge burning tires on the road from the south to Tehran, and my mother's new shoes were furtively slipped underneath an iron curtain after Khomeini had called for strikes. Despite all the difficulties they now look back on and laugh at, they were happy, and soon began making a life for themselves. After stints in Tehran and Mashhad, my father became a respected engineer and architect making 'good money', and spent his weekends skiing on the slopes of the Alborz Mountains. My mother, on the other hand, was working part-time in a cultural centre previewing films before they were screened in cinemas, surrounded by members of the country's intellectual and artistic elite; in short, they were both doing what they loved, had prestige, and were financially well-off. They weren't forced to leave, nor did they do so unwillingly: they did it for me, for a son whose tomorrows they wanted to ascertain.

* * *

But to return now to the heart of the matter: the mountains. As the capital of Iran, Tehran boasts many iconic landmarks – the Shahyad (now Azadi) Tower, the Milad Tower, the Golestan Palace; but none, perhaps, are as embedded in the history and soul of the city – underneath its skin, as one would say in Persian – as the mountains. Remove any of the aforesaid edifices, and you'd still have Tehran, as bustling and beautiful as ever; without the mountains, however, Tehran as one knows it would cease to exist. Looming on the horizon with their snow-capped peaks, sometimes visible through the miasma of smog that often engulfs the city, and at others vague masses in the distance, they stand proud and resilient, unmoved by the vagaries of brutal time, as old as she herself. While many unfamiliar with the city and country assume it to be, on account of its geography, a barren wasteland of deserts, to paraphrase Sir John Chardin, Iran is a land of mountains, *kuhestan.* Since time immemorial, the Aryan tribes who migrated from Central Asia atop horse-drawn chariots have been cradled by the mighty Alborz Mountains in the north, and the Zagros Mountains in the south. Across the latter do the Bakhtiari tribesmen make their perilous journeys to their summer and winter pastures, and through the former pass avid weekenders to the shores and villas of the Caspian Sea. It was by the skirts of these redoubtable ranges that empires were formed, maintained, and lost. Men may move, but mountains do not; while the children of Cyrus have seen Iran ravaged, passed between the hands of her many suitors, conquered, and reclaimed again, the mountains have remained ever standing, keeping a silent vigil they shall break only on Judgment Day.

* * *

I wake up one morning to the sound of crows cawing on the dusty branches of the ashen-coloured trees outside. I look at myself in the cracked mirror on the chestnut dresser, notice my growing beard, and think how much it suits me in my present surroundings. I turn my head left and right, keeping one eye focused on the mirror, fancying my profile bears an uncanny resemblance to that of Cyrus the Great (or rather, his posthumous depiction). Striking a match and lighting the little gas stove in the kitchen, I prepare a pot of tea, yearning inside for my grandmother's shiny *samovar,* which she'd keep alight, even throughout the sultry summer days that afforded no respite save the zephyr from the feeble air conditioner above our heads. I scald my thumb,

Joobin Bekhrad

damning Heaven and Hell, as I pour myself an unappetising glass, and flick through the few available television stations disinterestedly. Stern warnings from the Koran alongside images of the *Kaaba* in Mecca, imitations of Western game shows, domestic football matches, macaroni advertisements – the day is off to a rather vapid start. Then again, however, I have little else to do, and pinch my nose in vexation at the thought of having to stay for another two-and-a-half weeks. *Khodaya, be dadam beres:* God, where art Thou?

It's not that Tehran is a drag – it's anything but, really – but rather, that I'm far from being at home in this city. Unlike most of my friends outside Iran who have scores of relatives and close friends there, and dig the whole *mehmooni* business, I come from a comparatively small family, have very few close friends, and have never really been one for traditional gatherings, let alone the city's infamous parties that implode behind closed doors. I don't have to tell anyone there that I'm out of place; it's almost as if they can smell it, detect it from afar – perhaps in the same way that I can tell if someone is Iranian from observing their gestures from miles away. Without even having to speak, and make known my 'Armenian' accent (according to my grandfather), I'm dead on arrival, branded a *khareji*, an outsider. I dress and walk differently; I don't have a bandage on my nose, plucked eyebrows, or an electrically charged hairdo; I'm calm, and in no hurry; and I look at everything inquisitively. To make matters worse, both my first and last name – despite being as Persian as you can possibly get – are not very common, and I'm often told I don't look Iranian. *Where are you from? Are you Iranian? Are you sure? You don't look Iranian. 'Joobin' – is that a Persian name? Hmm …*

It's quite a strange sensation, really, feeling like a stranger in one's own country. 'Abroad', in Toronto and London, I feel Iranian – or at least, 'Eastern' – almost to a fault; nearly everything I consume, the places I go to, and the people I associate with have something or other to do with Iran. As well, being a [proud] member of a visible minority, my 'Iranian-ness' becomes incredibly pronounced, and I constantly look to let people know about my ethnicity and talk to them about the culture and heritage of my ancient, magical homeland. In Iran, however, I'm just another Persian guy with bushy eyebrows, facial hair, a *farvahar* necklace, and a big nose; all the exoticism dissipates along with the romantic feeling of exile and having something to 'fight' for. Well, at least my name is still, strangely, unknown to many Iranians, and I apparently don't look very Persian. Oddly enough, many would be happy to be in my situation: who wants to be considered typically Iranian, when they could be mistaken for an Italian, Greek, or Spaniard? One could even play along with the misconception: *Iranian? Moi? My mother's Italian, and my father half-Spanish, half-Persian, baby.*

In the process, my 'Western' identity rears its head, reminding me that perhaps I'm not the lovechild of the East I so often like to fantasise about. Just as the Samanids in the tenth century yearned to hear again the sweet sound of Persian recited in their courts after the 'Two Centuries of Silence', in Iran I long to hear – and speak – the English tongue in all its bastardised glory. I miss the amenities and luxuries I often take for granted; I miss the way things once were, and long to return ... *home*. In the West, I yearn to go back to Iran, and feel ostentatiously Iranian, while in Iran, I feel undeniably Western. I'm a stick with shit on both ends, as is said in Persian.

Yea, in the city where the streets have two names, I'm an outsider, a foreigner, and at times, goddammit, a tourist. The only memories I have of this place are those of lazy summers and prolonged business trips, my grandmother's little apartment on thirty-second street in Shahrara, the labyrinths of Zafar, cool evenings by the foothills of the mountains in Darband, Western Atefi Street by the Park-e Mellat, and getting lost in the Grand Bazaar. I don't remember the War, the eighties, *Kolah Ghermezi*, or *Madreseh-ye Mooshha*. I never did military service, never had to take a nerve-wracking national exam to enter university, and never for a second thought about the uncertainties of the morrow. I'll never have the honour of saying I'm an Iranian – born *and* bred.

Yet, I still consider Iran home (in a strictly figurative sense), and, despite always leaving with a sense of alienation and a heavy heart, long shortly afterwards to return there. No matter how many journeys I make to Iran, and no matter how disillusioned I become, I know I'll soon tire of the plush comforts of the West and desire to make, once again, for the Alborz Mountains and the land of *gol-o-bolbol*; for Iran, no matter how much she vexes me, brings me to tears, and wrings my aching heart, will always be my motherland, my solace, my saviour.

* * *

I miss, more than ever, that bustling city with all its beauty and squalor, serenity and madness, jarring contradictions, and awe-inspiring grandeur. I miss the smell of roses, on paper and in the parks, and the sight of faded tulips strewn across the decaying façade of a highway mural; the taste of hot tea in my grandmother's house, and the sound of Golpayegani bellowing forth from her crackly gramophone; the sight of the mountains on a crisp spring day, a cool northern breeze rushing through my locks; the smell of saffron, crackling *esfand,* and exhaust, all at once; the taste of pomegranates and rosewater; and the feeling of standing on the shoulders of giants.

I once read in a book that 'Tehran' is Aramaic for 'The Place to Which I Shall Return'[1]. It's not only

Joobin Bekhrad

I who long to return there, but also everyone I know who has had the chance to visit, however briefly, that metropolis nestled within the mountains in a most ancient land, Iranian and *khareji* alike; never, perhaps, has a city been so aptly named. Tehran, from thee I hail, and to thee shall I return …

12/3/2015

Bibliography

1. Farrokh, K. *Shadows in the Desert: Ancient Persia at War.* Oxford: Osprey Publishing, 2009.

A Requiem for a Nose

A twelve-year-old Iranian boy in 'Tehranto' looks into a bathroom mirror one sultry afternoon in July. What does he see? Two swarthy, conjoined shrubs nestled comfortably atop two glowing brown eyes, silky down aplenty, an intractable mane with a life of its own, and, surrounded by it all, the *pièce de résistance*. It is his birthright, a legacy passed down unto him from generations past, the protuberant mark of the heirs of empire and revolution. Fingering it with moist digits exacerbated by the relentless summer heat, he feels its bony ridge and pudgy end. He notices how its appearance varies depending on whether viewed from the left or the right, and how it takes on different shapes as he tilts his head beneath the flickering bathroom lights. He has his poses all sorted out, knowing that even the slightest nod here or there can spell photographic abomination. His is a love-hate relationship: he acknowledges his nose being such an essential part of his identity, yet loathes it at the same time. Standing there, he remembers having heard something about noses and ears being the only parts of the body that continue growing throughout one's life. *It's all down the toilet from here*, he thinks, zipping up his trousers with a sigh, and giving his appendage a final squeeze.

* * *

I often found myself as a child scrutinising my face before mirrors – in the loo, in stores, and any other place that had them – and comparing it to those of my classmates. I longed to be just another ordinary 'white' kid with dull, stringy hair, unassuming eyes, eyebrows far removed from one another, and, of course, a 'normal' nose – whatever that meant. Naturally, from my parents' perspective, I had it all; according to them, the other kids all envied me, and, deep down, were only jealous that the gods hadn't blessed their lacklustre physiognomies with such refinement. I would have the last laugh, in the end, when everyone else would be bald in their thirties, and I'd still have a thicket to run my hands through. I had 'character', they said; did I want to be just another run-of-the-mill kid, going about my business unnoticed and unheeded? Well, yes, in a way. My mother's encouragement-cum-consolation didn't help in the slightest, but rather made things even more difficult to deal with. 'They're idiots. All the best-looking celebrities have had thick eyebrows. Just look at Sean Connery!' But I didn't want to look like Sean Connery or his doppelganger, Ayatollah Khomeini – I just wanted to look like everyone else, and later, like a rock and roll star. Hell, Ziggy Stardust didn't even *have* eyebrows.

During my teenage years, I took comfort in the fact that, had I been a bit older, I might have been able to pass for one of the Gallagher brothers. Their eyebrows were just as bushy as mine – if not bushier – and their noses weren't exactly small (though I wasn't sure whether to attribute that to bust-ups or genes). I could never wait for Liam and Noel to pop on the television during my summer holidays in London. 'Look!' I'd tell my grandmother, 'there's the guy who looks like me'. For whatever reason, I was endlessly looking for people and things to associate myself with, and with whom I could create some sort of bond. George Harrison became my favourite Beatle on account of his Eastern-looking eyes and eyebrows, and Ronnie Wood a snouty Stone to aspire to. I felt as if we all shared something in common, and that theirs was a circle in which I fit in and had a place. That's all a teenager is really looking for, isn't it? Somewhere, something to call their own – a 'tribe', a gang, whatever. I belonged to the club of big noses and facial hair: a club Groucho Marx wouldn't have minded joining, perhaps.

For better or worse, my days of wallowing in imagined kinships with British rock and roll stars came to an end when university started. I had already come to terms with my fabulous nose and eyebrows, but, as I began to reconnect with my roots, not only further embraced them, but took pride in them as well. Though only superficial, they were yet visible signs of a culture, nation, and heritage I felt privileged to belong to. I stopped plucking the few hairs between my eyebrows and started sporting stubble, as I felt it added to the 'look'. Even though I still loved them, I stopped ogling pictures of the rock and rollers I'd grown up with, and instead began comparing my appearance to those of dead poets and pre-Revolution film stars. Despite my 'foreign' looks, it was always difficult for people – Iranians included – to tell I was Iranian; I wanted to set the record straight, and the nose and eyebrows that had once unsettled me became tokens I flaunted with élan. 'What do you mean I don't look Iranian? Just look at this nose, honey!'

* * *

The unflinching affection I hold for my Iranian nose – and the Iranian nose in general – is not shared by as many of my countrymen (and women) as I'd like to think. I've perhaps put things too lightly; *the Iranian nose is under attack.* Yes, many an Iranian nose has fallen prey to petty insecurities and wholly foreign notions of beauty. If many of my female Iranian classmates had put up with their beautiful noses as teenagers, they hacked them off as soon as *baba joon* had let them. It isn't only the nose that goes under the knife, though; off go those eyebrows and that unsightly peach-fuzz, too. And who needs eyebrows when you've got devilish-looking tattoos? Let's get rid of all your bodily hair, actually, and bleach your locks a nice platinum blonde. And those lips? They need more 'oomph', *azizam!* We'll doll you up real good, sweetheart – so good, people won't even notice you're Iranian.

My mother always used to tell me that Iranian women were amongst the most gorgeous in the world. Why, then, have I seldom encountered any women I find attractive on the streets of Tehran? Call me old-fashioned, but blonde beehives exploding out of headscarves and Botox just aren't my bag. Everywhere I look for my beloved Iranian nose, unadulterated and unscathed, but alas, in vain. Pint-sized bumps have taken the place of those beautiful twists and turns, and in lieu of the lips so eulogised by poets, engorged masses of hot pink. In state television dramas, the story is less outrageous, but more or less the same: pretty things whose only claim to fame is their green and blue eyes. The stations streaming from 'Tehrangeles', on the other hand, are but freak shows of the extremities of plastic surgery. Why, for as long as I can remember, have Iranians wanted to distance themselves from their true selves? Why is, 'Really? But you don't look Iranian!' today intended to serve as a compliment? Cyrus the Great is rolling in his grave – and rightly so.

* * *

At times, when I find myself sitting in this or that café in Tehran or Tehranto, I wonder if the Iranian nose as I know it is dead altogether; so much of it has been hewn away that it is beyond recognition, a sort of cartilaginous palimpsest. Indeed, so rare has the Iranian nose in its unsullied form become that it now excites me, oddly enough.

Joobin Bekhrad

Upon encountering an Iranian woman with a natural nose who doesn't have one foot in the grave or has just come from the sticks, I'm solaced by the thought that perhaps all is not lost, and that there's hope for my generation yet. At the same time, I remember my mother's words, and wonder when one of those gorgeous women is going to stick her big, beautiful Iranian nose into my life.

7/10/2016

Something Better

I slip through cracks, I burn holes. I slide between fingers, rip asunder the night. I speak in hidden tongues, nestled between dusty pages daubed in the ink of the unseen. I am guided by the undulating spirals of knowing eyes and the soft depressions of my mind. I tug at the fringes of shadows, ever in pursuit of the memory of light. At times this light seems so palpable, while at others, I have to squint hard enough to remember its warm orange glow amidst that black nothingness. Smothered in cinders and ash, I am known by many different names: they call me Khalil Oghab, Daedalus, the one that got away. Others, like me, have been burned, and some, beaten. *Illegitimi non carborundum*, I say. There is always a way out, always an aperture to squeeze through. I am an escape artist.

* * *

Under this roof, I will tell you about flowers, the stars, the night sky …

Somewhere, in a remote corner of the Persian Gulf island of Qeshm in southern Iran, have a covey of people made their homes[6]. Certain objects strike one as familiar: refrigerators, carpets, valises, jugs of water. Perhaps, aside from the

---

[6] A reference to Gohar Dashti's *Stateless* series (2015)

people themselves, they are the only things one can establish any sort of relation with. What are these towering masses of sand and stone? The ancient bed of a sea that once was, most probably; but they look too perfect, too human, to have been the result of chance and geology. They remind me of the crumbling ruins of Nain and Abarqu, two other dots out in the boondocks forgotten by God and man alike, synonymous in Iran with 'the middle of nowhere'. *Where the fuck is Qeshm?* Does it matter? What is significant is that these people have been driven here with only the shirts on their backs – and in some cases, not even that. A camel lies dead on the parched earth, its hooves fettered; elsewhere, a man lies huddled up in the foetal position upon a roughened mound. Shrouds of black have been tossed upon the sand, and the *Pietà* is echoed in the hollows of a grotto: the death, presumably, of the past? The dromedary's corpse reeks of foreboding; death and decay here do not herald a rebirth of any sort, but only the beginning of the end. Their only roof, the sky, their only bed, the hard earth, ablaze beneath the sun and frigid in the moonlight. On the other side of the world, in some stuffy club in Greenwich Village, a corkscrew-haired beatnik who tips his corduroy cap to Old Bob is whining words through his nose; but he doesn't know 'how it feels', does he? He doesn't know anything about these woebegone wights in godforsaken Qeshm, or those little Syrians sleeping with the fishes.

No one can tell for sure what has brought these people here, and why they've had to flee their homes; and, as with the whereabouts of Qeshm itself, it doesn't matter. Famine, war, natural disasters, *whatever* – we only know that the journey won't be the last they'll make. Whether they'll have to drag their feet to some other wretched place again, or rove within the folds of their minds and create, somehow, a mock imitation of their past lives, they'll never know a moment's peace. Once uprooted, forever uprooted. New soil will invite them to wither away, God knows where, while the old soil – transformed, evolved, changed – will never be the same. Only its vestiges shall remain, if not devoured by time. The camel shall not rise again, let alone pass through the eye of a needle.

* * *

I don't know much about Ahvaz, other than that my maternal grandparents lived there for a while, as did my paternal ones, owing to their connections to the army and the Iranian Oil Company. My father never cared much for it, having always preferred nearby Abadan. Come to think of it, nobody in my family had a particular affinity for Ahvaz; they just, owing to circumstance, happened to find themselves there, and had to make the best of things. I suppose it wasn't all that bad. Sure, there were the occasional sandstorms, swarms of locusts, and the stifling heat that would melt the pavement beneath one's shoes; but there were also ice cream sandwiches, *noon khameii,* and rivers of black gold.

Whatever happened to Ahvaz and Abadan, those cities in the land of the Khuz? Yes, there was 1980 'and all that', and both are still standing proud beneath the Iranian and Brazilian flags alike; what I mean to say is, what happened to the Ahvaz and Abadan of my parents' childhood? Tucked away beneath my bed are shoeboxes full of photographs of old ghosts and relatives. I've never been to southern Iran, but I can tell the thick Polaroids taken in Ahvaz apart from the others; those cream-coloured brick houses and empty expanses are dead giveaways. For my relatives and I, though, they're little more than miniature visual aids that shine every which way. Our memories are fuzzy to begin with, and, as such, they don't exactly help elucidate things any further. Has our Ahvaz, the only one I've ever known, been lost forever? What if there weren't photographs to smear and play with in the light?

* * *

In Berlin, there is a bottle[7]. Its shape is peculiar, and resembles something between a clothes hanger and a pomegranate. It looks like it belongs in some sort of sanatorium rather than someone's flat, and as if its contents are waiting to be consumed,

---

[7] A reference to Anahita Razmi's *Air d'Ahvaz* (2015)

perhaps through injection or inhalation. There aren't any holes or perforations; nothing can enter or exit the apparatus. Contained within it is not any balmy Teutonic air, but the air of Iran, of Ahvaz, deemed to be amongst the most polluted in the world; and, suspended in that air is not only the ancient dust of Khuzestan and exhaust, but also a million images, smells, and sounds of yesteryear and millennia past. It is the common thread linking mighty Elam, the armies of Darius the Great, d'Arcy, and Mum's cherished ice cream sandwiches. As long as the delicate glass object isn't smashed to bits, the prized *air d'Ahvaz* will remain pure and unsullied for centuries to come. Its proud owner can rest her head on her pillow and take refuge from the frosted streets of Berlin in the glowing warmth afforded by the bubbled breath of her homeland.

I have grown up surrounded by bubbles, bottles, and other such receptacles. I have even lived in them myself, for they are some of the many heirlooms that have been bequeathed unto the Iranian people.

* * *

Something told Grandpa he had to leave. Epithets like 'Cat Killer' and 'Hanging Judge' just didn't sit well with him. He didn't like all that talk of 'us' and 'them', about blasphemy and righteousness and the stains of depravity and decadence that had to be wiped off the soiled face of Iran for good. It was all too familiar; he'd heard it all before, and didn't want to sit around to see how things would unfold. He remembered the stories his father had told him about the Russian Revolution, and how, as a child, they'd made his hairs stand on end. Poor Sheykh Kazem! How could he have guessed on that cool April's eve in Badkubeh that he'd walk out onto the cobblestone streets below to find them awash, in the morning light, in every hue of red? How happy they'd all been after hearing of the fall of the Tsar; the Russians, everyone thought, would pack their bags and quit sticking their noses in everyone's affairs, once and for all. Little did they know that they'd come marching back again in those shiny black boots with renewed vigour, ready to sink their teeth into Iran once again and tear it into pieces. White? Red? Same old, same old. The bastards didn't have mercy on their own mothers; how could anyone expect to remain unscathed, especially Sheykh Kazem – the 'Master of Merchants' – with all his choice wares? Damn the heavens! What enmity did God have with that beleaguered trader? *First, my cartons of glass, smashed to pieces on the shore,* he thought, *then, my loads of tobacco, scattered in the snow – and now, this!* Ah, if only the great Mirza Kuchak Khan had been there to lay down the law of the jungle; but no, Khaloo Mirza was busy kicking ass in the besieged forests of Gilan. Alone and destitute again, amongst the infidels – O, poor Sheykh Kazem! God bless your soul!

If it hadn't been set in stone, Grandpa made sure to hack it in himself. They would leave Tehran for London at the first opportunity. Why would they leave Tehran? Because 'they' were coming to get 'them' – of that Grandpa was sure. He didn't make any distinction between vermillion coattails and greasy, swarthy beards. They'd snatch everything they had from them, he thought; yes, they'd eat the rich alive! And why, out of all the places on earth, would they make for pitter-pattering London? Because his brother, *Amoo* Mohandes, a.k.a. *Agha Dadash*, was living there in Hampstead. Tehran for the Tehranchians was no-man's land. As with my father's side of the family, Grandpa was too conspicuously tied to the old 'idolatrous' regime, and if the *pasdars* didn't come looking for him sooner or later – or so he thought – it would only be a matter of time before a neighbour or old 'friend'-turned-revolutionary would tip them off. Perhaps it wasn't as much of a conspiracy as he'd thought, though; someone, for the sheer hell of it, reported my family to the authorities. To Grandpa's fortune, and the displeasure of the nefarious individual, the venerated name of Sheykh Kazem – may God have mercy on his soul! – saved the day.

Just as Sheykh Kazem couldn't have imagined that he'd wake up to see Badkubeh infested with Bolsheviks, neither could Grandpa see then how his life would forever change. The move to London wasn't just physical; it wasn't only a land he had left behind, but also a life. In Tehran, the names of him and my grandmother had carried weight; they had *meant something*. In London, they became Mr and Mrs T., the quaint Iranian couple with the Persian rug doormat, from whose windows often came the smell of *sabzi polo*. They didn't have anything against the English, but just couldn't dig George Michael and *Black Adder* (Freddie Mercury was a different story), or wrap their tongues around their language (why even bother when they spoke that of poets?). There wasn't really anything quintessentially 'English' about them altogether, come to think of it; like those trees in the desert, they'd been uprooted, and had to try, somehow, to make do with their new surroundings. My grandparents' way of doing this, I suppose, was to recreate their apartment on Tehran's Vozara Street. You won't see it marked on any maps, but, in a little flat, just a stone's throw away from Marx's grave (poor Sheykh Kazem!), can be found in north London, proper and prudish, a little Iran. There, the only voices heard are those of Hayedeh and Shajarian; within, one sits on Persian rugs, flowery and faded, burning their tongues on hot cardamom-infused *chai* that's been brewing for an entire morning, beneath the languid gazes and arched eyebrows of bare-chested Qajars. On the living room table can always be found pistachios – which, although nowhere near as tasty as those from Rafsanjan, satisfy the palette yet – powdery sweetmeats, and a decaying volume of the odes of Hafez. While it may be difficult to decipher the gilded curves in the frame hanging above the sofa, all you need to do is ask, and Grandpa, assuming the air of the Bard of Shiraz himself, will reveal its meaning: *Wash thy prayer rug with wine, should the old Magus deem it fine.* Telephone calls are answered with a 'So-and-so *jan*, can you hear me? *Alo?*', and doorbells with a '*Befarmaid*'. More often than not, it's Auntie who's come for lunch, or my cousin Shahrzad, to give Grandma the uncensored lowdown on Iranian high society in London, brimming with all the juicy, sordid details.

They live in London, but they don't. They live in Tehran, but they don't. Where do Grandma and Grandpa really live? When they left their apartment on Vozara Street, Grandpa wasn't thinking about stuffing any air into bottles, or pickling any mementos; he didn't need to. In London, their little flat would become a bottle itself, a living, breathing memento, a capsule of the life they'd left behind and in which they would relive their memories: a work of escape artists *par excellence*.

* * *

My grandparents didn't *want* to become escape artists; they *had* to. As did I. What else could I do, down on my knees in suburbia? A volume of poetry strikes a chord; before you know it, you're digging through your old schoolbooks again, tracing the confounding dotted letters with your fingers like a blind man, cursing the very idea of abjads and taking a stab at what vowels might lurk between those thick black swirls. After reading stories of Daddy-o and his bread, you start developing a thing for Behrouz Vossoughi and the fuzzy-wuzzy black-and-white sixties flicks that never fail to jam right before the belle in the miniskirt takes to the stage. You hang around *chelo kababis*, become addicted to tea, and ask your mum what the hell Shajarian is *chah-chah*-ing about. Your parents tell you you'd be better off reading about how to make money and hit the big time instead of the *Tuti Nameh*, the *Chahar Maghaleh*, and other books 'no one reads', but it all goes in one ear and out the other. You do it because your heart and mind are somewhere else, because the world outside has always been so cold and strange, and because there's no place you'd rather be than the hearth of your mind, of your soul, where moustachioed *lutis* fall in love with prostitutes, bards sing of lovers to the twang of the *dotar*, and *daevas* are damned. You do it because as an Iranian, it is an instinct, an impulse surging at once through body and mind. It is the legacy of poets, lovers, and punks alike.

* * *

Daqiqi did not love the world he lived in; or, rather, the world did not love Daqiqi. The House of Sassan had crumbled, but its memory lingered yet. The land of the noble had been smothered in billowing black shrouds, but shining beneath could still be seen gilded swathes of deepest purple and red. The vicissitudes of cruel time and fortune had humbled Daqiqi into submitting to the new world order, but had failed to extinguish the flames of love for what he most held dear: *the ruby-coloured lip, the harp's lament, the blood-red wine, and Zarathustra's creed.* If only he'd yearned for less! Perhaps then would he have been able to bring his masterpiece to completion. O Ferdowsi, poet of Paradise, the world reveres thy hallowed name. But what of you, Daqiqi? You longed for the ruby-coloured lip, but were murdered by a Turkish slave. Like Hallaj before you, you paid for your tongue with your head.

Other children of the night, born of darkness and silence, fared better than Daqiqi. They spoke in allegory and metaphor, in riddles and rhyme. Veiled beneath flowers and musky ringlets lay the hidden meanings of their words, sometimes stupefying, always sublime. The 'beloved' could have been a damsel, or, more likely, a page, depending on how one saw things; and, perhaps bulbuls and hoopoes really were *just bulbuls and hoopoes.* Unorthodoxy and free-thinking were seldom presented as such, often being clothed in the austere raiment of faith. Man and God, one and the same? *No, no – he was speaking of an earthly beloved – bite thy tongue!* In any case, those who went against the grain did so in the footsteps of Daqiqi. Khayyam and Razi (how well the two would have gotten along) managed to evade their detractors unscathed, as did the drunken Bard of Shiraz, although all were labelled heretics. The pages of Hafez's *Divan* are soaked in wine, the wine of the Magians, of the tavern, of ruins. Was it all mere allegory and a matter of aesthetics? May I be struck dumb! Hafez didn't long for the temple's flame and the ways of the wine-imbibing Persians of old. No! Wine, the Magian Elder, the tavern – they were only metaphors! Hafez – God forbid – couldn't have been a closet-Zoroastrian and a toper – or could he? Hafez, you sly genius, you. *For eternity hath the Magi's ring been on mine ear; we are those who were, and them shall we forever be.* Legend has it that upon his death, Hafez's critics were reluctant to give him a proper burial on account of his 'heresy'. To put an end to their quandary, they opened a page of his dripping *Divan* at random, and were met with the following lines: *Turn not away from the bier of Hafez; steeped in sin, he shall enter Paradise!*

Needless to say, Khajeh Hafez of Shiraz was soon interred within the life-bestowing earth of Shiraz. He had his cake, and ate it, too.

* * *

Some punk at an underground Tehran rave probably has it in his head that he's a badass hoisting high the flag of the 'burnt generation'. Intoxicated by music, coke, and the lascivious glances of the pretty girl in the corner licking her lips, his high is intensified at the thought that he's managed to get away with it all, right under everyone's noses. He is there, in his subterranean sanctuary, feasting his senses in a way that would make even those in 'Dobai Dobai' and 'Tehrangeles' salivate with envy. *Tehran isn't such a bad place, after all,* he's thinking to himself, wiping his nose and feeling a hot bulge in his trousers. What he doesn't know is that this isn't *his* legacy, or even that of the romanticised burnt generation that thinks it's seen it all; he's merely the heir of the countless Iranians before him, who, through their genius and artistry, managed to fashion worlds for themselves removed from those they knew. And, what that 'badass' also fails to realise is that in place of the whip and the electric shaver, his forefathers once trod beneath the shadows of gibbets and blades.

* * *

Tell me – without you, what stream shall quench the desire of parched lips?
Without you, in what breeze shall I seek a refuge from my weariness?

Googoosh is on the television again; but 1970-something is long gone. It must be a clip from a videotape, perhaps pulled from the magic bag that is the Iranian supermarket, or something stumbled upon by chance on an LA station[8]. Googoosh is singing about a separation gnawing at her, eating away at her being; without her beloved (God? Saeed Kangarani? Some hypothetical figure sprung from the pages of Persian romance?), she simply cannot find the strength to carry on. The title of the song, *Hejrat*, recalls the flight of the Prophet Muhammad and his followers from Mecca to Yathrib (later 'Medina') in 622 AD; other migrations, however, are implied by the scene in question: the flight of the Shah from Iran in 1979, the flight of the family itself, the flight and disappearance of a life once led. The members of the family have gathered around the television in silence; not a word is said, or needs to be, as they can all intuit each other's thoughts. Everyone is thinking the same thing; *Khanum* Googoosh's words are only adding to their pertinence and poignancy. Heads are slightly titled to the side, and displeasure and nostalgia meet in their expressions. A sarcastic huff is imminent, as is the dreaded lump in the throat. How can they go on living without Googoosh, especially when she herself is speaking of her own despondency? Should they, like Googoosh, 'weep as long as they live', and see 'happiness die before them'? Neither did Googoosh do that, nor have they done so. Like my

---

[8] A reference to the cover artwork for Sholi's *Hejrat* album (2008), photographed by Michael Aghajanian. In the photograph, an Iranian family in the diaspora (most likely in Los Angeles) sits watching Googoosh singing *Hejrat* on the television in their living room.

grandparents, they have created a little Iran of their own, replete with Persian rugs, démodé rococo sofas, Googoosh, and all. They have yet again worked their wonders as escape artists, in the spirit of their forebears. There may be a glass receptacle in Berlin filled with the blessed air of Ahvaz; but it is merely one of many. Tehrangeles, Tehranto, 'behind closed doors' in Tehran, my grandparents' flat – what is the Ahvazi specimen in comparison to these animate bubbles and ampoules?

Once, a few years ago, a friend of mine invited me to his place in Rudehen, a small town on the outskirts of Tehran. I didn't know what to think. As with Qeshm, the only thought that popped into my mind had to do with Rudehen's obscure whereabouts and an expletive; I could have been on my way to Abarqu, for all I knew. So be it, I thought. If I was going to enjoy a day away from the hysteria of Tehran, it might as well have been in the sticks.

Rudehen was – as I, a typical Tehrani, had imagined – underwhelming. My friend's pad, on the other hand, came as a welcome surprise. When describing Rudehen, my friend had spoken of stars in the night sky and nature's bounty; a little oasis wasn't exactly what I'd been expecting. We had Indian food, listened to electric blues, discussed the oil paintings on the wall, and reclined on cushions adorned with the face of Forough Farrokhzad. I could have been at a friend's in London, if only I'd forgotten about Rudehen and the little mosque down the street. I actually began to like the idea of living by myself in a sort of secluded capsule, far from the pandemonium of the big city, doing whatever I wished in private. *My own private Rudehen,* I thought to myself, laughing at my own words and wondering what on earth had happened to Keanu Reeves. Just as I'd fashioned my romantic little world of Persian poetry, folk epics, and *Film Farsi* heroes as a way of bearing the boredom of the 'burbs and my uprooted state, so too had my friend created a getaway for himself as a means of dealing with a world he didn't find as welcoming as he'd liked. Staring at a cushion, Forough's pretty face melded with that of an artist friend back in Tehran; her words took on a new significance, and rang as clearly as ever in my ears. I could picture her in her studio, fanning her sweating self in the midsummer's heat and flicking away the ashes of a burning cigarette: 'Don't think we're the majority here, Joobin *jan.* We're living in a bubble we've created for ourselves.'

* * *

The verses of Daqiqi and Hafez. My grandparents' flat, and my friend's in Rudehen. The air of Ahvaz, bottled up for centuries to come. The 'hearth' of my mind. They all belong to different times and places, but have all been necessitated by one and the same thing: the longing for something more, something *better*, as a flaxen-haired Faithfull once sang. Whether we have moulded our bubbles owing to physical displacement, in response to the unforgiving Fates, or as a result of the fear of dogma and orthodoxy, we have done so instinctively, evoking the spirits of our ancestors and in true Iranian fashion. The bastards – whoever and *what*ever they may be – will forever try to grind us down; but when all is said and done, we know that we will always slip through those cracks and slide between those fingers: we, Iranians, of the burnt generation and golden years, of centuries of darkness and silence, of the wine-drenched land of the noble.

5/17/2016